To

D Florida Hospital College.

May our stories inspire the
Readers of this book.

Warmest Regards.
   Barenise Potter.

Venete Klein

Executive Director, Absa Bank Ltd

Foreword: "Look at Me"

Bringing new hope, new thoughts, and new respect for the unknown, are the manner in which I came to know Marlene Le Roux. Sharing my heritage as a proud woman from the "Cape Flats", I find this amazing person a force to be reckoned with when it comes to spearheading the cause of those who are sometimes ostracised by society due to our ignorance.

Our paths crossed a number of years ago and I was stunned by the immense aura of positive energy that engulfed me and the people Marlene interacted with. It was only when I looked closer that I realised that this young, beautiful woman suffered a disability. Through my interaction with Marlene I realised that this is one individual that did not allow her circumstances to define her, but that she is a strong woman who rose against all odds. What is more enlightening is the fact that she inspires others with disabilities towards a level of self acceptance and pride. This book, called "Look at Me", is but one of the significant examples of how Marlene is mobilising us, and others with disabilities, towards realising the beauty of God's creations.

I recall the first time that I was given a copy of this book, compiled by Marlene; I was lead to tears on a flight back to Johannesburg. I could feel how my fellow passengers were staring at me. I could not be bothered, because as I read the stories, I experienced a divine moment of pride for women who blossomed against all odds and did not allow themselves to become just a statistic within society. At that moment I decided that these stories need to be told, the beauty of women needs to be amplified, and the uneducated needs to be educated.

It is with this in mind that I made a conscious decision to become a fellow custodian of the message of hope and beauty that this compilation of stories resembles. With the drive for inclusivity within Absa, and me being the Executive responsible for driving the disability agenda, it was not a tough decision to make to become a sponsor of a re-print of this book. Meeting with a selected group of the women, featured in this book, has made this partnership invaluable as these ladies make it their

calling to be forces of significance within their respective communities. The message out there is simple and clear – disability does not mean inability. Disability is considered the unspoken of and is hidden within many of our communities. However, this book has managed to confer a message of hope. The captivating stories of hardship and misconception of 23 South African women, who are drawn from different backgrounds, shows that sheer grit, determination, and hard work can change anybody's self-imposed realities.

This inspirational book should become an iconic means through which we must continue to educate and empower our communities to reach new levels of understanding and respect for those less abled than ourselves. Just because somebody sufferers a disability does not make them less intelligent or less beautiful. I urge you to think of those around you and make a contribution to the community that you live in by reading this book and sharing in the pearls of wisdom encapsulated in these stories. Think about how "You" can contribute to improving life for people around you. Or how can "You" put a smile on someone's face today.

In conclusion, reading this book makes me draw from the wise words of Maya Angelou, who says:

"You may write me down in history with your bitter, twisted lies; you may tread me in the very dirt; but still, like dust, I'll rise.

Absa and I consider ourselves privileged to be associated with this formidable project.

Venete

My original intention with compiling the book was to show women with disability in an empowered way.

The responses to the book surpassed my expectations within the broader public. Not in my wildest dreams did I imagine the broad spectrum of views that it unleashed. Not all responses were positive, but I achieved a public debate on mindsets that triggered either enlightened responses or total conservative viewpoints.

Even in the disability sector, the book shaped mindsets to think out of the box.

For the women in the book it is still an exhilarating experience.

This book has spoken to persons beyond disability. It confronts the reader to find the humanity in each other.

I would like to thank Venete Klein for having the vision to implement the second phase of this journey.

Marlene le Roux

Look at me

Compiled by Marlene le Roux
Photographs by Lucie Pavlovich

I started with this personal journey six years ago. I approached numerous publishers to buy into the idea of depicting women with disabilities as sensual beings. Somehow they did not get it. This just made me more determined.

I realised from a young age that society puts people with disabilities in a box with an *ag-shame* attitude. I just felt I want to celebrate who I am, disability and all. I realised that only a person with a disability can change the mindset of society.

There is a great lack of publications which highlight or address the positive stories of disabled people in general and, more particularly, women with disabilities.

These stories allow women to reflect on their struggles and their inner journey to personal self-mastery, the painful discovery of puberty, rejection and the overall victory of *I am* and *I am beautiful for me*.

This publication is intended to affirm not only women with disabilities, but all women. Every woman who has asked herself who am I, or tried to tailor herself according to the acceptance of others.

While compiling this publication it dawned on me that the road to self-acceptance and sensuality is painful and challenging every single day. Being born with a disability or encountering a disability later in life are two different journeys, but equally challenging.

Celebrating yourself as a sensual and sexual being, when society expects you to exist only according to their perception, is a path only a few are willing to undertake. During my research I interviewed various women with disabilities who were not yet on the road to self-acceptance or were simply striving to be 'normal'. They just wanted to fit in with society.

This publication was not an easy task. All 23 women, including myself, had to face places and things which we had successfully masked simply to survive. It was a painful and healing process for all of us.

Due to the multiple disabilities of the women, their active participation was a production within itself, from writing their stories to the careful planning of the photo shoots. Here I would like to applaud the remarkable team I worked with from project manager, publishers, photographer, to logistic team, make-up artists and hairstylists, who all believed in this vision from the start. Their passion and tireless efforts kept me going in the moments I wanted to give up.

Again I realise that life is not just about the individual. An individual's dreams and aspirations can only be realised with the help and the belief of other people.

Finally, the stories of these remarkable women should be inspirational to parents with children with disabilities, to encourage their children to start celebrating their lives.

Compiler

Marlene le Roux

We have always believed in pushing the boundaries when it comes to new concepts for books. When Marlene le Roux approached us with the idea of a book featuring beautiful, sensual, disabled women, we knew it was a project we wanted to become involved in.

For far too long disabled women's sensuality has been hidden, locked behind the doors that protected society's view that a disabled woman could not be beautiful. That she was somehow less of a woman than her able-bodied peers. "Look at me" aims to challenge this myth. Disabled women are women first. Beautiful, sensual, sexual women who want to be treated not with pity, but with admiration and respect, like all other women.

It was a privilege to work with each one of these wonderful women. They are truly an inspiration, having conquered so many of life's challenges with grace, dignity and self-respect. We have decided not to do much editing to their stories. We wanted their voices to be heard loud and clear. It is, after all, their lives and their stories of triumph that make this book such a unique publication.

Genugtig! Publishers

On behalf of the City of Cape Town I am pleased to endorse the reprint of Marlene le Roux's book "Look at Me". We are proud to be associated with this initiative to promote awareness of disability issues. We also seek to promote awareness of the forms of support that are available to people with disabilities, including Dial-a-Ride, subsidised municipal services, and an ongoing programme to make City buildings wheelchair friendly.

The City first got involved with this thought provoking project when we commissioned the French Exhibition "Estetique & Handicap" in 2008. I am thrilled to see that Absa has taken on the reprint of this book that celebrates the sensuality and sexuality of disabled women. I am sure that it will offer a new perspective to many of its readers.

I would like to thank all those involved especially Marlene le Roux and the management of Artscape for their continued dedication to making Cape Town a cultural awareness capital in South Africa and the world.

CITY OF CAPE TOWN | ISIXEKO SASEKAPA | STAD KAAPSTAD

THIS CITY WORKS FOR YOU

Alderman Dan Plato
Excutive Mayor
City of Cape Town

This edition is dedicated to the memory of the late Soraya Scott who demonstrated to the world that despite her disability she still led a complete life.

Contents

Barenice Peffer

Cerebral palsy

I was born on 25 December 1963. My parents were very excited when my mother went into labour on Christmas day and gave birth to a beautiful baby girl. I was born at home with the help of a midwife and I seemed to be a healthy baby. When I was about four months old, my mom noticed that I could not sit up. She took me to a doctor, but he downplayed it and did not think much of it. As I grew older my mother raised her concerns again and this time the doctor told her that I was just a slow developer and that they would do an IQ test when I was two or three years old.

At the age of two I could still not walk and I was referred to the Red Cross Hospital for physiotherapy. I was diagnosed with cerebral palsy. In layman's terms this meant that I was brain-damaged. They classified me as a spastic diplegic, meaning that my legs tightened up with spasms, which resulted in me walking with difficulty. It was a big shock for my parents, but when an IQ test was done when I turned three, the results came as an even bigger shock. According to the doctors, not only would I be disabled for the rest of my life, but I would also suffer from mental retardation.

The doctors advised my parents that the best thing they could do for me was to put me in an institution, because I would never be able to live a normal and productive life. They also told my mother not to have any more children, as they would most likely also be disabled. My mother refused to listen and went on to have three more babies – all perfectly healthy. She also never put me in an institution.

As I grew up, my disability was never a problem for my friends. I enjoyed participating in sports and games with them. It was only when I became a teenager that some adults would negatively refer to my disability.

One day a friend of the family made a remark that I would have been a beautiful girl if I was not disabled. I remember how shocked I was when I heard this. I decided not to let it get to me and to go on with my life. During my teenage years I went through the same stages of development as my friends, even having crushes on boys.

One day I was talking to an aunt and I told her about my dreams for the future. One of which was to get married. When she heard this, she made the following remark: 'What man would want to marry someone like you?' I was shocked and could not believe that she could be so cruel and heartless.

The fact that some people were negative about my disability started to have an impact on my self-esteem. I felt that I was not beautiful because of my disability. I had this idea in my head that as a disabled woman, no guy in his right mind would find me attractive. It took me years before I decided that I was not going to allow ignorant people's attitudes towards my disability to rule my life. I started to celebrate my womanhood and the fact that I am a disabled woman.

I was 18 when I met a guy from Durban and he became part of my life for more than ten years. When I met Jay I immediately felt attracted to him and he seemed to feel the same way. I met him in January 1982 in Paarl. After the holidays he returned to Durban and we started to correspond with each other. He started phoning me. Later the phone calls became more frequent and he would phone three to four times a week. I was always looking forward to his calls and could not wait to get home after school so that I could be home when he phoned. I remember how my heart skipped a beat whenever I heard his voice. When he told me he loved me I was in seventh heaven. I thought that for the first time in my life someone actually loved me despite my disability.

During those ten years he would promise to visit me, but he would never turn up. I came to the conclusion that he was playing around with me and I decided not to speak to him again.

I felt disillusioned about love and decided to focus on my studies. As a disabled woman I also wanted to be economically independent and I felt that I had to educate myself and get a degree. When I entered university I made the decision not to get involved with guys again.

It was during my third year at university that my life took a new turn. Just before the new academic year started I received a call from a guy called Eugene. He was calling from Johannesburg and said that he needed information about the special school in Cape Town. I was not in the mood to speak to a stranger about special schools and told him to write me a letter detailing his request. Eugene sent the letter and later phoned me to ask if I had received it. Later that year during April 1989 he came to Cape Town for business. We hit it off immediately and I felt very comfortable with him. After our first meeting, I received a bouquet of flowers from him the next day. I was very surprised because it was the first time that I had received flowers from a man. During the week that he was in Cape Town he told a friend of mine that he was in love with me, but I was not impressed when I heard this because I did not believe in love at first sight. I told Eugene that I was not in love with him, but was prepared to be friends with him.

We were in constant contact with each other and I saw him again a few months later in August, when he asked me to be his girlfriend. At first I was reluctant because of my past experience but he did not give up and I finally agreed to the relationship.

Eugene really knew how to make me feel special, even though it was a long-distance relationship. He would send me flowers on a regular basis as well as gifts by post. Whenever Eugene came to Cape Town he would wine and dine me and spoil me with gifts. Our courtship was really a wonderful and exciting time for me.

Two years after we met, Eugene proposed to me and I accepted. I knew that he was the man that I wanted to spend the rest of my life with. We were engaged for three years before we got married.

We were married on 18 December 1994. We decided to wait a few years before we started a family. Everything became easier with Eugene in my life, and because he was disabled too, he always understood my feelings and we could support each other. People are always surprised when they discover that Eugene and I are married, because it is very seldom that they meet disabled couples.

After three years of marriage we decided to start a family and in January of the next year I discovered that I was pregnant. We were very elated about the fact that we were going to be parents. My pregnancy went well and I gave birth to a healthy boy. When people came to visit us, the first question they would ask was whether Stefan was normal. Our response would always be that he is definitely *not* normal, because he has blonde hair and blue eyes, unlike either of us!

Eugene is a wonderful father and he helped me so much with our baby. After five years I became pregnant again, but unfortunately I had a miscarriage two months later. A year later our lives would change forever, as I became pregnant with not one, but two babies! We were going to have twins.

I became more and more aware of my physical limitations as the babies grew inside me. I had to use a wheelchair for the last three months of the pregnancy. I would not have gotten through my pregnancy without the help and support of Eugene. I managed to carry the twins full-term and they were born on 7 July 2004. We had two healthy babies.

I feel so blessed to have gone through this journey of pregnancy. I never realised what inner strength I had until I had the twins. I loved being pregnant and felt beautiful. Stefan is now eight years old and the twins — Marushka and Larissa — are three years old.

Becoming a mother has completed my journey into womanhood ...

Profile

Qualifications:
I attended the University of the Western Cape where I graduated with a degree in Library and Information Science (B.Bibl.Ed.). I am a qualified librarian and a qualified teacher, although my passion is libraries.

Occupation:
At present I am working at Helderberg College in Somerset West as a librarian and am the head of the media department as well as a classifier. I have been working at Helderberg College for six years.

Hobbies:
I enjoy watching tennis and ballroom dancing. I also enjoy cooking, reading and meeting interesting people. I am a member of the Library and Information Association of South Africa, as well as the Association of Seventh Day Adventist Librarians.

Contact details:
email: bpeffer@hbc.ac.za
tel: 021 850 7593
cell: 084 337 1431

Barenice's album

ttle me

Sexy me on the beach

Me as a sports woman

Eugene, our beautiful son, the twins and me

Our wedding day

I am Bonita, a woman made in God's image, born to be different, a reflection of perseverance, an echo of the power

I am Bonita — a woman, a daughter, a lover, a friend and a sensual creation of God's supreme hand. With shrieks of loud excitement I came into the world on Saturday, 9 January 1982. Firstborn to my parents who received me with open arms and thankful hearts. Me, a small bundle of humanity, untouched by prejudice and unaware of the shadow of darkness that would hound me for life.

Blindness descended upon me at the age of four months, silently robbing me of the chance to experience a Capetonian sunset, to view the Mother City from the top of Table Mountain or to see the beauty of my mother's face. Yet I took it in my stride, since you cannot miss something you never had.

That was 25 years ago and since then life has turned out to be a voyage in and out of myself. I journeyed from being a blind baby, to being a blind toddler reaching out to foreign objects with eager hands. I then blossomed into being a blind girl, with ponytails and matching ribbons. My teenage years were mild and sweet without too much temperamental mood swings. And then, like a ship on her maiden voyage, I cruised into womanhood.

How can I ever describe the feeling of utter horror that swept over me the day I realised that people thought of me as less of a woman just because of my blindness? Suddenly, I wasn't allowed to be what I wanted to be. My dreams and aspirations weighed less than that of my seeing counterparts.

How could I, Blind-as-a-bat-Bonita, aspire to be a journalist or dream about having my own talk show on radio? All of a sudden I was confronted with stereotypical notions and ignorance from a world that thought of me as crazy. Who gave me the right to want to be a part of this so-called 'normal world'? I had to be boxed in, trapped by social apathy and conventional beliefs; and of course I wasn't satisfied with being just another disability statistic.

I got my degree in Journalism through hard work. Dragging my poor mom through countless academic libraries, while my dad waited outside, practising the patience of a saint. I took the challenge to make my dream a reality, not because I wanted to be a social show-off, but because I needed to be recognised as a person in my own right.

The academic hurdle was not the only one I had to overcome. My blindness automatically got me classified under the 'She won't be a good wife, girlfriend, mother or employee' label and not even my degree could tip the scale in my favour. I was blind, therefore I was deemed unable to experience red-hot passion or breathless ecstasy. My feminine instinct to want to feel loved, treasured and desired didn't matter.

These words are a true reflection of my life. The constant battle to prove myself, despite my blindness. Kind of like an infomercial:

'Viewers, I present to you the Bonita Model. She can cook, clean, make love, have babies and do the washing. All despite her blindness! Isn't that amazing? You can have her absolutely free, all you have to do is to accept her the way she is!'

The journey still continues and I fight the battles with the same fervour with which I love. I suppose it is the small print on my birth certificate, that little clause nobody knows about, except me and women like me. The clause that states that we'll constantly have to prove ourselves.

I am Bonita, a woman made in God's image, born to be different, a reflection of perseverance, an echo of the power He gave me to claim my right to be!

Profile

Qualifications:
I matriculated at the Athlone School for the Blind, and got my B.Tech. degree in Journalism at the Cape Peninsula University of Technology.

Occupation:
I am currently working in the Eskom Communication Department, and I am a qualified journalist by profession. Journalism always held a challenge for me, because of my curious nature and passion for writing. Words are my obsession; I live for the thrill I get after I have completed a poem or a short story.

History:
I worked as a journalist in the Cape Talk and KFM newsrooms, and also worked as a presenter at Bush Radio, 89.5. My experience in the radio industry taught me the importance of communication. It was great to interview people who made a difference within our country, province and communities.

Contact details:
email: bonster@ravemail.co.za
cell: 073 415 2572

Bonita's album

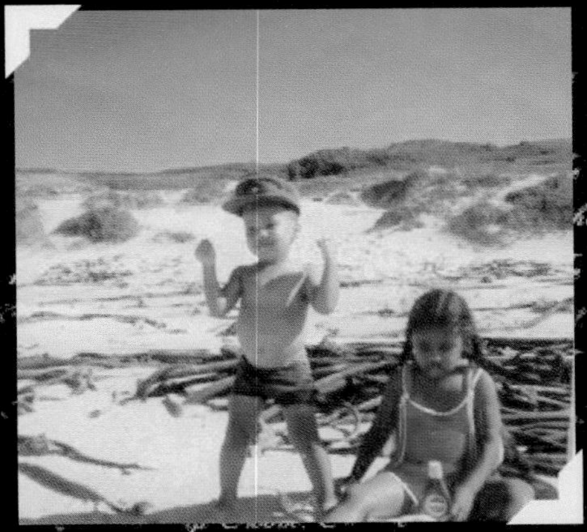

At the beach

At three I contracted polio. At four my mother gave me away. I am the product of an affair.

« A trois ans, j'ai contracté la polio. A quatre ans, ma mère m'a abandonné. J'étais le fruit d'une liaison amoureuse sans lendemain. [...] Je n'avais le droit de participer à aucun sport à l'école. Je me rappelle les cours d'éducation physique pendant lesquels je devais rester de côté et regarder l'entraînement des enfants valides. »

Mariée, trois enfants.
Achève son master.
Sept médailles d'or, six médailles d'argent et quatre de bronze en tennis de table aux championnats de la Province du Cap.

Claire Franzman
polio

At three I contracted polio.
At four my mother gave me away.

I am the product of an affair. My mother's husband left her as a result of my birth and she was destitute. My biological father did not leave his wife for my mother so I travelled between my father and his wife and a babysitter, until my mother gave me away to a couple in Wellington.

I can remember the day very clearly. It was a late Sunday afternoon. My mother stayed in Matroosfontein and she brought me to Wellington. My 'new mom' took me for a walk and when we returned, my mother had left. I remember sitting down in the backyard and crying. I had to teach myself to call these strangers Mom and Dad. As time went on, I thought less and less about my biological parents. I had new parents who treated me as their own.

My new father was a farm labourer and my new mother was a char. Our home had only three rooms and I had to share a bed with my new parents. We had no electricity; we did not know any luxuries. The only new clothes that I had were the callipers I received from the hospital because my legs were too weak.

Nothing was easy. It was my duty to fill a bucket with water for our household needs. The tap was outside the house. I also had to start my journey to school at 6.30 am every morning. The children teased me about my disability and I then resorted to using my fists. The teachers would not allow me to take part in any sports. I remember during physical education, I had to stand aside and watch the able-bodied kids exercise.

I was in Standard 2 when I first met my brother from my father's side. When I got home from school, he was there waiting for me. He told me that he had been looking for me for years. Apparently my mother gave me away to ensure that I didn't end up with my father. This was the first time I realised I had another family. Five brothers and two sisters.

The following Sunday my father arrived with his wife and my siblings. He wanted to take me with him to raise me, but my adoptive parents didn't want that. I kept contact with my biological family, even though my adoptive dad didn't like it much. He was scared my biological father would take me away.

After school I couldn't go to varsity due to financial constraints. I also had to stay in hospital for eight months after I had a procedure to lengthen my legs. I started at the Rehabilitation Centre for Disabilities in Athlone in January of 1989 and there I met two people who would have an immense influence on my life.

Mrs Bridgette van der Merwe was the person who helped me to discover myself. She especially helped me with all my issues regarding my adoption. She helped me to reunite with my biological mom. She taught me that if you open a pod of peas you get different sizes of peas, just like people. If you open them you find different characters and some are nice and some are not.

I was very scared the day I finally met my biological mother. I asked Mrs van der Merwe to come with me to the meeting. I didn't close an eye the previous night as I kept wondering what I should ask her. I didn't even know what I should call her. And what if the meeting failed?

When we got to her house in Mitchells Plain the following morning, I was very scared. A woman answered the door and called me Nicolene (that's my second name). She asked me to come in. Mrs van der Merwe said she would give us some time alone. I wanted to run away. The lady, my mother, told me that a woman never forgets her own child. I couldn't ask her any questions as the tears streamed down my face.

She went to fetch a necklace to give to me. She had kept it for me all these years.

Mrs van der Merwe returned after an hour. I still couldn't ask her any questions. So I returned to the centre with Mrs van der Merwe.

The other person I met at the centre was my first love. He was an introvert and I made the first move. I thought he was the most handsome man on earth, even though he was also disabled.

At first I didn't know how to catch his eye. So when the lady drew up the new timetable for cleaning the kitchen, I asked her to book me with the hunk I had an eye on. That was where it all started.

Our first intimate moment was in the library. It was my first big kiss. A new world opened. I had butterflies and could see bright stars in the middle of the day. Our relationship grew rapidly. I wanted to be with him every minute. Mrs van der Merwe was against this relationship. She said he would never be able to be a man for me.

Three months later I accepted a job in Paarl. He was upset at first, but I reassured him that it did not mean the end of our relationship. Our relationship grew even stronger. I phoned him regularly. He came to visit me on weekends. I always went to visit him on payday.

We first had sex in 1990. I will always remember it. I was so scared. I can only recall him telling me that he would be gentle. I gave myself to him fully. And one month later, I was pregnant. I was now more terrified than ever before.

I asked him to tell my parents. My father said that even broken trees carry fruit.

Three children were born out of our relationship: two daughters and a son.

We finally broke up in 2000 after he started abusing me. I refused to go through such hell. He had little self-esteem because he couldn't find work, so he turned to alcohol.

At the centre I also started enjoying table tennis. I joined a club called Miracle. In 1990 I represented Western Province in the SA Games for the Disabled. In 2004 I represented my country in Rio, Brazil, and now boast seven gold, six silver and four bronze medals for table tennis.

I am currently employed by Hawequa Correctional Services in Wellington. It wasn't easy to start with. I was the first disabled person to work there. I had to teach the other personnel to accept my disability. I am three subjects away from completing my B.Tech. degree via Unisa.

I have a wonderful, beloved husband. We both have had our fair share of sadness and now we try to prevent getting hurt again. He makes me feel like a woman and carries me on his hands. I wonder why he never came into my life earlier, but I know you first have to go through hardship to realise life isn't just fun and games.

I also realise as a disabled woman, when I listen to disabled men, that they think our private parts are also disabled or that we can't have a normal sex life. They just don't realise that we give so much more of ourselves to keep the men in our lives happy. I think other disabled women will agree with me if I say that we don't know the meaning of saying no to the man we love. Or at least, I am always ready for intimate moments with the man I love.

And as a mother, I am blessed with three healthy children. I always try to give them the best I can. I try to be a friend and role model. Just like other mothers, I try to protect their beautiful dreams.

Claire's album

With my table tennis medals

Qualifications:
I am busy completing my B.Tech. degree at Unisa.

Occupation:
I work for the Department of Correctional Services.

Achievements:
I have represented Western Province and have won seven gold, six silver and four bronze medals for table tennis.

Contact details:
email: claire.fransman@dcs.gov.za
cell: 083 500 9992

My children and I

« Lorsque j'étais sur le point d'accoucher, la sage femme à la clinique n'a pas voulu me traiter avec respect, j'ai alors décidé de ne plus avoir d'enfants. On m'a dit de porter plainte. Ce que j'ai fait, mais sans suite. »

Mariée, deux enfants.
Hôtesse d'accueil pour SA Port Operations.

Denise Petersen

Cerebral palsy

My name is Denise Petersen and I was born on 23 September 1964 in Cape Town, in a township called Bishop Lavis.

I was born with cerebral palsy and developed anxiety disorders.

My father passed away and left my mother, a domestic worker, to care for her seven children alone. I was nine at the time. Life was not so easy. She never remarried. I will always be thankful for what she did for us.

I attended Eros School. One of the highlights in my life was when I received the award for Overall Best Progress. I was also nominated as head girl of the school, but Eros only went up to Grade 10, so I had to leave. I went to work at the Palms Centre as a tea lady and a cleaner. I met with a teacher from Eros who told me Eros was going to start offering Grades 11 and 12. I did not hesitate to go back and finish my schooling.

During Grade 11, I started getting these headaches. The school psychologist decided that I would not be fit to do Grade 12. I was very upset, but did not give up. I told him I would be able to do it, and I did! This was once again my way of showing the world that everyone has the right to let their voice be heard.

I was introduced by a friend to a special person. I knew nothing about him; he was very shy, and did not talk to any young ladies. I did not know that we were both in the New Apostolic Church. I wanted to go to church with him and this is how we became friends. I did not have any romantic intentions, because he was an employee at the school and I was in Grade 12 and head girl. It would have been improper for us to date. Time passed and things became very quiet between us until he just disappeared from my life.

I didn't care because I had many other male friends who never thought of me as being disabled. They just respected me as a special friend. I liked to chat to everyone. That's how I met a guy who eventually became my lover. He had another pregnant girlfriend and he even asked me to marry him, but I refused, and that was that.

Out of the blue, the shy young man who disappeared from my life appeared again. Our friendship grew intense and we started dating. In August 2008, we will have been married for 17 years.

We didn't want to start with a family right away, but unfortunately I fell pregnant after only two months of marriage. I was shocked, but my husband was delighted. It was difficult telling our parents. I was so shy. But I had to, because my sister couldn't wait to tell everyone. It was Christmas time and when I told them, they were overjoyed.

I had a very healthy pregnancy with no hypertension or difficulty in walking like other women when they are expecting. I carried my baby full-term.

My husband, who is a general worker for the Education Department, took out a housing subsidy in order to buy a house. I was working for R100 per month as a teacher's aid because I couldn't find any other employment. When I wanted an increase, my employers refused and told me that my work wasn't good enough. The teacher, however, felt otherwise, and I felt discriminated against, but I kept my faith.

I became pregnant with my second child during a time when I was very depressed. Again, I had a very healthy pregnancy and I also carried full-term. I had normal births with both my kids. I did not need any special treatment.

When I went into labour, the midwife at the clinic did not treat me with respect and I decided then and there that I did not want any more children. They told me to lay a complaint against the sister. I did, but nothing happened.

I am presently doing contract work. In my job I come across many able-bodies who see me as a threat. They will, for instance, not show me how to do the work, because they want to be paid for their knowledge. But I never give up. There are good people everywhere. I have a colleague at work who cares very much about me; he is always prepared to go the extra mile for me.

My husband is an able-body. He is no angel – make no mistake. We've had some ups and downs in our life, just like any other married couple, but we are married happily. He cares for me and the kids. He gets up at 4 am in the mornings to help me get ready for my transport that sometimes arrives at 5 am. He even takes off my shoes when I need him to do so.

We put our money together and we pay our debts together. When we got married he did not know how to cook or bake. While I was ill in bed, he had to cook. I was lying in bed and I guided him. Now he can even dish up the food and wash the dishes. He also does the washing and ironing of my clothes when I am unable to. When anyone falls ill, he takes leave from his work in order to take us to the doctor. We do everything together, even walking to and from church. He is a minister in our church and sometimes he must stay behind after the service, but he will first walk me home because we don't have a car.

My kids are over-protective like their father, they always make sure that there is nothing that I can slip on. When I come home from work, even the kids in the road run to help me if there is no one at home to help me.

We have a very strong belief in our religion. We are a God-fearing family. We have trust in our church ministers. If we have any problem in our house, we do not run to our parents; we go to our ministers for advice, no matter what the problem is.

Like the palm tree that can survive any weather, that's how I see myself; whatever trouble comes my way, I will always stand up against it.

Profile

Qualifications:
I completed Grade 12 at Eros School and was head girl. I did a learnership in Mail Handling at SA Post Office and in Business Administration at SA Port Operations, and a course in Customer Care and Occupational Health and Safety.

Occupation:
I am a clerk at SA Port Operations.

Hobbies:
I enjoy singing in the church choir, cooking and baking, visiting the sick and flower arranging.

Contact details:
email: denpeter@pgwe.gov.za
cell: 083 740 4246
tel: 021 397 1356

Denise's album

The big 21 ...

BRIGHT SPARKS: Eros School's matric achievers: (from left) Denise Abels, Patrick Michaels, Roger Benjamin, Berenice Mitcham and Soraya Pienaar.

Five bright pupils leap matric hurdle

oud Eros pupil

My wedding day!

My family

Donna Abrahams

Born with no right hand

One day she tested me – as she often did. She gave me slices of bread to hold. After the sixth slice, there was no more place on my arms to pack it. When she handed me the seventh slice, I quickly realised that I needed to make a plan, so I opened my mouth and in went the seventh slice! That's how my mother ensured that I fully adapted to the world. She played such a big role in my self-acceptance.

The lesson I learnt from all her little tests is that I might not follow the same pattern as others in doing things, but in the end I could perform them just as well. After all, where there is a will, there is a way.

'Once everyone around you accepts you for you, it will be easy for you to accept yourself,' she taught me.

It was hard for her to see her child struggle to do things that should have been a breeze to do. Some days she would watch me and reach out to help, but just as she gave up hope, I would come to her and say, 'Look Mommy, I did it.'

Sometimes I struggled to understand my mother's tough love approach. I now understand why she did it – she never wanted me to accept that anything was impossible. The concept of 'can't' did not exist for me.

I was born without my right hand … For any parent it is the happiest day when they welcome their newborn baby into the world, but nothing can prepare a proud new mom and dad for the news that there is something wrong with their baby.

At first the children at my primary school had many questions about the girl with the one hand. Some of them were cruel, but they soon got used to the idea that one of their friends was different. I did at times hide my hand, but was encouraged not to do so. I must admit, I didn't feel different. Yes, I had one hand, but I could laugh and run and jump like all the little girls of my age. I was more protected than the rest of my siblings – so much so that I did not have the privilege to go to pre-school.

My brother and role model says that he remembers me as a strong-willed, determined little person. This is because I never saw myself as someone with a disability and this gave me confidence.

Once I came to terms with the fact that I was different, I became more confident and used this to my advantage.

He thinks I would have been right-handed as I still have the tendency to attempt everything with my right side. As a baby my bottle was held snug between my chest and my stump, and I became very frustrated when I couldn't do things with my right 'hand'. Time forced me to learn to use my left hand. Today I am ambidextrous, because I have good coordination with both my left and right side. My brother says

I am an inspiration to many, including him, because I have overcome a challenge.

Later, like any young person, I too became aware of my physical appearance. I remember that at one stage I was extremely aware of the lack of a hand. It was then that I thought no guy would be interested in me. To my delight and amazement the boys started lining up like they do for any other girl. But I gave them the cold shoulder! I developed a bad case of the 'what if' syndrome. 'What if' they were only feeling sorry for me? 'What if' they only wanted to prove a point? Any journey has some bumps. It is only once we've gotten through all the bumps that we actually realise what we have learnt from the journey.

The journey to womanhood was taking it's toll.

There was one guy, Leon Abrahams. I remember my first thought was that I really did not like his surname. The strangest thing is, he didn't even realise that I only had one hand – he just liked me for me. We were married in 1997. I felt like a princess. I didn't want the day to end.

The most beautiful part of my life followed. My three pregnancies. I had Brandon in 1998, Liam in 1999 and Tyra in 2000. Just like all other women, I also had the usual pregnancy fears as time drew closer for me to give birth to my first child. No, I did not fear that my 'disability' was genetic. It was something much simpler – I feared that I would drop my baby when I bathed him! In the hospital they teach you how to bath your baby using two hands. Just thinking about it made me stress. When I eventually bathed my first baby, it was one of the many proud moments of my life. After that first bath everything else fell right into place.

I survived a society that takes one look at you and labels you. A society that does not understand that it is the ability of the person that matters; not the disability. Therefore it still saddens me when I see people being discriminated against or if I am discriminated against because of public ignorance to see past a so-called disability. I was recently discriminated against when I had to pass my PDP (Public Driver's Permit). The doctor doing the medical exam took one look at me and decided that I do not have full control of my vehicle. Needless to say, I was devastated and angry!

The day I got my civilian license was a proud day for me, as I never thought that I would be able to drive a manual car. I am, however, determined to go pass out for my PDP and I will get it. Every day I get behind the wheel, I feel extremely proud.

Parents have the tendency to get embarrassed when their children stare at my stump, or ask 'What happened to that auntie's hand?' I like it when they ask – how else will they know what happened to my hand?

Children really do say the cutest things. A little four year old once asked me if I forgot my hand in the washing machine. I thought it was the funniest thing on earth. My son, Brandon, was three years old when the kids at his crèche started asking questions about his mom's hand. All he said was, 'That's my mommy's bonga' and ever since, my stump is referred to as a bonga.

Profile

Qualifications:
I studied Art at Cape College. I worked for the City of Cape Town, in the department of Sport and Recreation. My work entailed youth development, community projects, family festivals and team-building programmes. I would say that creating murals and banners is a strong point for me. I was also responsible for an anti-graffiti campaign in the Mitchell's Plain area. For the past three years I have been involved with Special Olympics South Africa. I am a registered coach and volunteer in the organisation.

Occupation:
I am currently freelancing, teaching young artists in the Bellville/Kuilsrivier area.

Hobbies:
Scrapbooking, photography, swimming and crafts.

Contact details:
email: donna.africa/4@gmail.com
cell: 072 247 2553

Donna's Album

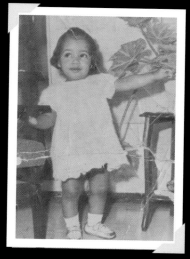

Some things never change

My wedding day

My three lovely children

I sometimes have technicolour dreams running through my mind, of the day before the accident and my life as an able person; now, as someone with a disability and all the challenges this brings, it is a fascinating movie.

« Est ce que vous vous êtes déjà demandé ce que votre vie serait sans l'usage de vos jambes ? Je n'y avais jamais pensé, jusqu'au jour où je me suis retrouvée sur un lit d'hôpital, incapable de sentir ou de bouger mes jambes. [...] Je n'aurais jamais cru qu'un accident puisse être aussi grave. [...] Que je suis naïve ! »

A obtenu le premier niveau du diplôme de Sciences de la Communication (Université d'Afrique du Sud).
Responsable administrative chargée d'Education pour « JSE Limited ».

Emilie Olifant

Paraplegic

Have you ever wondered what it would be like not having the use of your legs?

I never thought about this, until the day I found myself in a hospital bed unable to feel my legs or move them …

There I was, approaching my 30th birthday, having just managed to be debt-free; I'd bought my very first car and was making new exciting career plans. I thought I had my life under control. My future perfectly planned. Everything was working out so well.

In high school I took part in athletics and excelled in the 100, 200 and 800 m, running bare feet à la Zola Budd! In my spare time I attended karate classes and ballroom and Latin American dancing and took part in sport and extramural activities. I cherished health, athletics, travel and adventure. I went to the gym three times a week and like most women, I was obsessed with the toning of my stomach and thighs. All of these were building blocks that moulded my young adult personality. My identity and self-esteem had been based on the physical world. Looking back now, I can say with the knowledge of hindsight that before my injury I was lost, spiritually.

Everything changed when the doctor told me the news: 'Your spinal cord had been dislocated on the T11/12 vertebra level.'

I had been injured in a motor vehicle accident. I never knew an accident could be this severe. I had somehow imagined one could break a leg or an arm; sustain minimal bruises or scratches. How naïve of me!

When a catastrophe happens in life, it is easy to feel sorry for yourself. Everyone around you seems to become 'invisible', but healing starts through building and rebuilding personal relationships. Lessening personal misery comes with a sincere focus on what your family needs and the needs of other people around you. Not always easy to do! It saddened me to see how broken my mother, siblings and family were and it took a while before I realised I needed to do some soul-searching in order to eventually be content with where I was in my life's journey.

I knew that I needed to love myself more, before even attempting to look for love elsewhere. I met some awesome souls who invited me to dance along, so I made a conscious decision to get busy with the little things like cleaning my home each day, so I could invite anyone to share a cup of my herbal tea with me. I was also blessed with a wonderful friend who was very supportive of me during my traumatic time. Kgosi played a pivotal role in my life ever since I met him in 1999 and he really ran my outside life for me when I was in hospital. He was there – sorting out accident claims and police statements, offering moral support and giving me peace of mind. He was the middleman with my employers, updating them on my condition and recovery. He was truly my guardian angel personified.

Moving on with my life with a disability meant facing the future and those unknown lessons in coping with alien challenges. A very scary and nerve-wrecking prospect! Learning that I would not walk again was devastating, but I knew that I had to strengthen my state of mind and think positively for emotional and physical healing to take place.

When you lose the functioning of a muscle, that muscle becomes weak and loses its tone. My thighs lost some of their tone and my self-esteem was crushed. I was back to square one, having to work on the toning, and with more hard work this time as there was no automatic functioning of the muscles. I worked very hard at physiotherapy and weight-lifting programmes during my days of rehabilitation. I completed my three-month physiotherapy programme in six weeks. During occupational therapy, I learnt all about domestic and practical techniques for daily living. I focused on what I needed to know and what I needed to do to be content and happy within myself.

I thought about returning to work and hanging out with my friends and family as before. Then it hit me! The doctors could not predict the future for me and could not tell me to get used to the wheelchair. I had to figure it out for myself and I had to stay positive.

When I returned to work, I could see just how touched and inspired a lot of my colleagues were. For the first time, I realised there were a lot of people in my company who really liked me. The wisdom given to 'treat others as you would have them treat you' really counts when it matters most. Staying conscious with my inner self helps me to listen to what my body is telling me. I am certainly enjoying the lessons as they come. Whatever I am meant to learn from all these experiences, I am discovering daily.

I feel privileged to have been able to return to work. I resumed my job of managing and administering the JSE equities trading system and Safex examination. This involves preparing coursework and examination papers for equity traders and compliance and settlement officers. I try to do the things that I used to do before as best I can now. I became one of the members of the Employment Equity Forum, representing staff with disabilities, which I facilitated before joining the JSE Education team to focus on investor education. My aim is to increase understanding about disabilities in the wider community. Although the Constitution offers a great deal of support for people with disabilities, society in general does not know much about our situation.

Every day I make choices that will help me be the best I can be. There are days when I wake up and wish things were different. My disability haunts me and my mind checks in every time to ensure I think about my situation. Patience is not a choice any more; rather, it is part of my daily life. I also find that whatever I do becomes more meaningful if I keep my sense of humour.

It's really not easy living with a disability or any situation that causes you to perform less than your best. This also relates to anyone without disabilities who finds themselves 'disabled' in a different way. The HIV/Aids pandemic impairs relationships and causes 'insurmountable' financial stresses: these are all kinds of debilitating challenges that permeate our very existence. But somehow we continue getting on with our lives, don't we?

I take great care of myself. I look really good and brave and people think life must be great for me and that I must be coping. This is true – most of the time. I recently learnt, and am still working on embracing this: while my mobility differs from most people, the real person behind appearances is simply another spiritual being going through a human experience! You and I are no different in essence. We laugh, cry, rejoice and mourn the same things. One of my choices at the start of each day is: My disability does not necessarily 'handicap' me in my quest for a successful day.

People with disabilities are often given labels, labels which we wear without protest: assumptions that we are 'different'; our lack of motivation to assert our personal worth regarding discriminatory salaries; that we struggle with inaccessible architecture and so on. What can we do about it? How about honouring and respecting everyone – on an equal footing? What disabling factors would disintegrate if we owned our personal power and expressed it in our daily lives?

On my release from the hospital, I started equipping myself by doing research on spinal cord injuries and recoveries. I think that if we want to be true to ourselves, finding answers to the most important questions of life is a process. The time it takes to make genuine discoveries and find true beliefs varies for every individual.

The victory over the inactiveness was a landmark for me. I also found the self-discipline to exercise even when I didn't feel like it. This is extremely important, because overall health and any hope of recovery cannot be achieved without it. I found the Reeve-Irvine Research Center website and contacted a doctor, also with a spinal cord injury, who answered my questions and continues to do so, whenever I need to understand a situation or condition that impacts on my injury.

One day I heard an interview on radio with a woman from California who teaches yoga for the Multiple Sclerosis Society in California. I called in and asked the producer to give me her contact details. I tracked her down to her hotel and we started making plans to bring the techniques to South Africa. In June 2006 I organised a yoga workshop and invited yoga instructors who were interested in working with clients with disabilities. The workshop was a success. I find yoga so relaxing for the body and it helps reduce my stress levels. When I run out of energy, there are techniques I can use to energise the body. I put more time into practising yoga, focusing on proper breathing and energising mechanisms. I started doing yoga to relax and eventually fell in love with the techniques, and made it my way of living.

Since the beginning of my new life, I have always wanted to be as 'normal' as possible. This longing applies to every aspect of living with a disability. It is always a challenge finding the right balance between managing my own needs and meeting my obligations to others.

The emotional extremes of adjusting to a catastrophic illness or disability range from suicidal despair to recovering an appetite for life. Somewhere in-between is a grey area of numbness. You don't really feel depressed but you don't get excited about anything either.

The experience of having a disability, particularly after having had an active life as an athlete and a dancer, has made me a more spiritually aware person. I don't focus on what I have lost, but rather on what I have. In some ways I have grown a lot more than I would have if this had not happened to me. This is a challenge that turns you into a more mature and focused person, and I'm humbled by the experience.

I love travelling and I was most concerned that I would not be able to travel as planned because of my injury. My life is more structured now. I have to plan ahead, rather than simply pack my bags and go as I did in the past, but I still go. In my second year after the injury I met up with a group of beautiful souls and planned a trip to Mozambique over a long weekend. Exciting plans were made and it was considered that I would need assistance throughout our visit as we'd booked to stay in the tents on a deck by the beach, in Ponta Malongane. It was a fascinating experience and one I will not forget for a long time. We drove to Khosi Bay border in groups in three cars and I used my car as it had more capacity to carry luggage. We pooled our petrol and *padkos* costs. It was a nine-hour single trip and I drove non-stop. I enjoyed that drive thoroughly. When we had to stop, it was to rest or use the restrooms. I wore a leg bag. It has a valve that you open and close to empty the bag when it is full with urine. This made life so much easier, more so because everyone was so understanding.

A willingness to be open to sharing disability issues opens doors for people to be more understanding and accommodating. There is really nothing to be ashamed of. It makes it easier for people to relate to us as long as we remain approachable and open about our circumstances.

The hardest battle for me has been overcoming my own fears. This is an ongoing process. Now I can share that with others through counselling and group life-coaching. I choose not to let the disability take control of my life.

While I was doing my research one night, I managed to track down a spiritualist medium in Brazil. Someone from my church told me that they had been to this medium two years prior and had had overwhelming success through healing. After doing more research on this spiritualist, I headed for Brazil on a two-week journey. His name is João de Deus, which means 'John of God' and he lives in a small town called Abadiânia in Brazil. I wanted to gain my own experience and I knew that whatever healing would come my way, could only be for the better. João provides free treatment from his small hospital-style sanctuary – 130 km from the capital Brasília. The centre, known as Casa de Dom Inácio, is open three days each week: Wednesday, Thursday and Friday. The medium João loses consciousness when he incorporates elevated spirit entities that then use his body to perform operations, treatments and cures of the physical and spiritual bodies. All who visit the centre may observe and participate in the proceedings.

On my return to South Africa, I felt content with my injury and situation as it was and understood that for physical healing to happen, I needed to heal from the inside first. I guess my healing was spiritual.

I remember what it's like to run. Memories are more precious to me now. Once as physically active as I am mentally active now, I used to enjoy dancing, travelling and outdoor activities. I still do most of them. Now I also sketch, paint, and indulge in creative writing and poetry more, to relax. I also do research on spinal cord injuries and recoveries, using my own progress as a case study.

I completed my first level of a Communication Science degree with Unisa in 2003. When injured in March that year, I was determined to complete my studies. I am currently studying towards completing the Advanced Programme in Counselling at Unisa, with the view to better serve my clients during group and individual coaching.

I am content with who I am and where I find myself. The choices I make help me deal with each challenge as it arises. I do not have to worry about the things I cannot change. God knew that I would be able to handle this challenge and that someone out there is waiting to benefit from my story. It has been four years since my injury and I have managed to regain my independence. I bought a more spacious house that is wheelchair friendly and also bought a car and drive myself wherever I need to be. I have achieved a lot in my short life and have conquered my fears and face my apparent 'limitations' with an iron fist.

I sometimes have technicolour dreams running through my mind, of the day before the accident and my life as an 'able' person; now, as someone with a disability and all the challenges this brings; it is a fascinating movie.

Profile

Qualifications:
I have completed various courses and obtained certificates in Counselling, Business and Time Management and completed the first level of a degree in Communication Science at Unisa.

Occupation:
I am an Education Administrator Officer at JSE Limited. I also do group and individual coaching and motivation and I do research on spinal cord injury.

Hobbies:
Reading, creative writing, travelling, theatre, entertaining and being outdoors.

Contact details:
email: emilieo@jse.co.za
cell: 083 985 9091
tel: 011 520 7126

Emilie's album

the one in the front

Me in my Zulu outfit

My dad in his shop

Me scuba diving

This is my mom

Through all these years I came to accept who I was and what I was all about. The fact that I was a woman with dreams and desires gave me a sense of wanting to do something with my life. I refused to feel sorry for myself and made a conscious decision to be successful in all aspects of my life.

Eulleen van Heyden

Osteogenesis imperfecta

This is a story of a woman born with Osteogenesis imperfecta Type III, better known as brittle bone disease, a rare genetic bone disorder. This is my story, the story of Eulleen van Heyden, who has, amongst all the challenges that we are faced with as women, the further challenge of a fear of falling. I have to prevent this from happening at all cost, as such an incident usually has devastating consequences. Between 1960 and 2003 I have undergone 18 bone surgeries.

As a child, I walked for the first time at the age of eight and used bilateral callipers and ring crutches. I was elated with my new-found independence, yet I was faced with the terrible reality of falling and the consequences thereof. And, of course, I have my accidents. Each time I fracture a bone, I am in tremendous pain, yet I have an overwhelming peace within me. I know that I have to move on past every fracture as I have had so many. After the most recent fracture in 2007, it took me seven weeks to recuperate, during which time I realised that whatever the doctors told me regarding my bone strength, it would not prevent me from leading a fruitful, joyous, rewarding life.

I am the sixth child in a family of seventeen siblings. We lived in Flagstaff in the Eastern Cape. Three of my siblings also had this condition but to a more severe degree, and they all passed away early.

I was placed in an institute for disabled children at St Joseph's Home, Cape Town at the age of three. This was due to a lack of proper medical care and the high risk of injury in a normal school. The positive thing about my time at St Joseph's was that I had excellent schooling and they taught us how to be independent and take care of ourselves. Unfortunately the downside was that I was far away from my family and it left me feeling abandoned and alone. I was extremely traumatised by

the separation from my family at such an early age, but it was only later in my life that I realised how significant this would be in my development as an individual.

Unfortunately, St Joseph's only provided education up until Grade 7. So, at the age of fourteen I was placed in the care of an aunt and her husband in Durban. They were total strangers to me, but the only family willing to take me in, as my parents had separated. I lived with them for a period of eight years until August 1973.

This was a very challenging period in my life, as I was faced with dealing with anger and disappointment. They made me feel like a burden who otherwise would have been an orphan. I was often scolded for being a 'cripple bitch'. I had to cook, clean the house and take care of their six children in return for their 'kindness'. I saw very little of my disability grant.

Through all these years I came to accept who I was and what I was all about. The fact that I was a woman with dreams and desires gave me a sense of wanting to do something with my life. I refused to feel sorry for myself and made a conscious decision to be successful in all aspects of my life.

In 1973, at the age of 22, I arranged for training at the Industrial Training Centre in Cape Town. There I acquired various vocational skills such as sewing, working with wood and clerical training. But even more important than my newly acquired skills was the sense of freedom I experienced. I was independent for the first time in my life and I loved it.

I decided to live life to the fullest and accept all challenges. I go to live shows and jazz clubs, travel and participate in sports activities. I am free.

Another highlight in my life was when I had to face my first bus experience as a passenger. Being only 97 cm tall, it was a challenge to board a bus on my own, with callipers. Would I be helped, be frowned upon or ignored? I once encountered a situation where I was openly harassed in a taxi on my way to work. It was a very humiliating and embarrassing experience, but mostly people are genuinely eager to assist.

One evening on my way home, a fellow passenger helped me off the bus. To my surprise I saw him again the next day, while I was buying groceries. He approached me and said: 'Hi sweetie, you're the lady I met on the bus.' I couldn't believe he remembered me, but he was so kind and even carried my groceries home. His name was Ian. We developed an incredible friendship. He was able to look past my disability and we became very close. He is very protective towards me and I will never forget one specific day at the beginning of our courtship when he became overwhelmed with fear that I might be hit by a car. All of a sudden he picked me up and ran across the road with me to prevent me from being knocked down. At that point I was angry at his behaviour, but today we have a good laugh about it, because it brings back good memories. We got married a year later.

Ian is still my best friend and a wonderful, supportive and patient husband; he fulfils me in every way imaginable. We have a 'normal' marriage in every sense, and yes, we do have disagreements and are faced with somewhat more challenges than other couples, but we have decided to make our marriage a success with the help of the Lord and be the perfect partner to each other. In the year 2001 we celebrated our tenth wedding anniversary with family and friends and we renewed our wedding vows. As we never had a proper honeymoon, we went to Dana Bay on the South Coast, and had a glorious time together.

People would expect someone in my position to be introverted and shy, but I love to travel and meet all kinds of people. Even before I got married I would make arrangements to travel to Durban and Johannesburg to visit my siblings. I would fly or travel long distances in various buses, sometimes up-country too. I had a friend who was imprisoned at Robben Island for many years, and I would even visit him every three weeks. On my first boat ride I was extremely nervous, but I love everything about travel, all that is happening around me – the different people conversing in their respective languages and being exposed to different worlds.

At my current workplace I am the only employee who makes use of a wheelchair. Our building is not wheelchair friendly, leaving me faced with many challenges. On many occasions we have meetings which I am required to attend. These meetings are held on different floors, which means that I must be lifted in order to attend. Luckily I have wonderful colleagues who are not shy to assist me whenever the need arises. As people frequently help me, I am constantly aware of God's awesome presence in my life.

Life is to be lived to the fullest and every opportunity is to be used. We must be of service to others and not be selfish with our own experiences. In this way, we enrich the lives of those around us.

Profile

Qualifications:
I completed Grade 10 at Wentworth High School. My work experience includes data capturing, jewellery manufacturing, financial administration, manufacturing of components for an engineering company and switchboard operations.

Occupation:
I have recently accepted an exciting new position at an import/export company.

Achievements:
I received a bronze medal in a 5 km marathon in my wheelchair.

Hobbies:
I provide counselling to women in life-altering situations and enjoy travelling, outdoor life, socialising, and watching sport and experiencing the joyous atmosphere.

Contact details:
email: ian@zipprint.co.za
cell: 079 502 9074
tel: 0215930752

Eulleen's album

My tenth anniversary ...

Celebrating my birthday

With my husband

I decided that I needed to go on with my life. I did not want to be in a position where my life was passing me by any more. I wanted to play an active role in it. I took a major decision to stop the medication I was on. Within three months of quitting my medication, I was feeling like myself again.

My name is Gillian; my friends and colleagues call me Gill.

I have been diagnosed with bipolar disorder, which is a clinical state of depression, for which I have been treated since a very fateful day in 1984. After that day I suddenly became scared of everything, scared of going out on my own; scared of life. I had never been a scared person before, but I became very anxious and where I was a very confident person before, I became very unsure of myself. I became disabled.

I still see myself as a beautiful human being and somebody who can still achieve a lot in life. Bipolar does not make me a lesser human being. I still have the same feelings and having been diagnosed has put me in touch with my inner self. I believe having the condition is part of my spiritual journey on earth.

I was born in 1960 and lost my mother when I was four years old. This was devastating for me. I grew up in Stellenbosch in the Boland and I started school in 1966 at Rhenish Girls' High School. I only attended the school for a year when the Group Areas Act came into effect. Our school was situated in the centre of Stellenbosch, which was then declared a white area, and we had to move to a school in a 'coloured' area called Idas Valley. Growing up in Stellenbosch and observing that I stayed in a different community made me think that 'white' people were different from 'black' people.

I remember that every night at ten o'clock a siren would go off. This was to ensure that Xhosa-speaking people were in their township, Kayamandi, and not in the 'white' area. If coloured or black people were caught outside, they would be arrested. I really struggled to understand this as I always saw all people as the same. I had a happy childhood and despite apartheid, I was fortunate to have a good schooling, as my teachers were all dedicated to their work.

I was in Standard 8 during 1976 when we took to the streets protesting against what they called Bantu education and the inequality in education in our country. I finished my matric year at Luckhoff High in Stellenbosch and was fortunate enough to be the first one in my family to go to university. My late father was very proud of me. He encouraged me to finish my studies and make a success of my life. I studied at the

University of the Western Cape, mainly because during the apartheid era a 'coloured' person was not allowed to study at a 'white' university without a permit. I am not sorry that I attended UWC as this is where I learnt what was really happening in our country. Through my friends on campus, I was exposed to different cultures and learnt that we were all the same. During the three years of my studies, I became involved with student struggles and was actively involved in various marches and resistance struggles against apartheid. I was educated about politics, women's issues and the struggle for equality. I was actively involved with organisations like the UDF (United Democratic Front) and the UWO (United Women's Organisation).

I finished my studies in 1981 and qualified to be a social worker. I had a bursary from the then Department of Coloured Affairs and had to work for them for three years to pay back the bursary. I only lasted for a year and a half as I could not work for the same government that was oppressing our people. At the department we were not allowed to share the same tearoom with our white colleagues and they were paid more, even though we were doing the same work. I left the department to go and work at a welfare organisation of the Dutch Reformed Mission Church.

The eighties were a very stressful period in the history of our country. Many of my friends were detained and had to serve jail sentences for their involvement in the liberation struggle of our country.

During 1984 I was fortunate that I was not detained, but I was not prepared for what was to happen in my life: I was violently raped. It changed my whole life. All my dreams were shattered and my life came to a standstill.

I was advised to lay a charge with the police, but I could not do so as it was too difficult to talk about it. Three months after the rape I went into a major depression, mainly due to fact that I could not talk about it. I was hospitalised for three months. During this period I became scared of life; I became scared of everything. I had to resign from my job as I was not emotionally stable enough to go to work.

Whilst in hospital I was treated by a psychiatrist and had therapy with a psychologist, but nobody told me what was wrong with me. I was put on medication for depression, not knowing that the medication had side effects. I felt like a zombie most of the time and it was like my brain was frozen. I could not think straight. After my stay in hospital I tried to recuperate at home for two years.

During this time I was advised to apply for a disability grant. I was also told that I would never be able to practise as a social worker. I could not accept this. The one thing that I have learnt from this experience is to listen to your inner voice and do what you want to do with your life.

After being at home for two years, I had to make some decisions about my life. I had two options: I could stay depressed for the rest of my life or alternatively I could go on with my life despite the fact that I had been raped.

I decided that I needed to go on with my life. I did not want to be in a position where my life was passing me by anymore. I wanted to play an active role in it. I took a major decision to stop the medication I was on. Within three months of quitting my medication, I was feeling like myself again.

I found a job and did not go for the disability grant option as I felt that I was a qualified social worker and the fact that I was treated for depression did not mean that I had lost my skills as a social worker.

This was twenty years ago. I felt that I had fully recovered from my first bout of major depression. I went on with my life and got married. I gave birth to a beautiful boy. But five years into my marriage, I had to deal with a very painful and stressful divorce and again I became very emotional and could not stop crying. I did not realise at this point that I was heading for another major depression. I decided to go and see a doctor, who immediately referred me to a psychiatrist. I was admitted to hospital – a hospital for people with mental illness. The doctor then made a diagnosis of bipolar disorder. Again I was put on medication, as I was told my condition was caused by a chemical imbalance in my brain. This time around the doctor explained the side effects of the medication in detail.

It was not easy to come to terms with such a diagnosis, especially since there is so much stigma attached to mental illness and psychiatric conditions. Many times people suffering from a mental illness are referred to as being mad and unstable. I have learnt to live with bipolar and accept it. I have learnt to manage it, by listening to my body and taking my medication.

I was fortunate to meet a female psychiatrist, whom I have been seeing for therapy for many years. She helped me a lot to deal with all my emotional baggage. Initially I used to have many dark mood swings, but that is under control now and I always try to look at the bright side of things. I count my blessings on a daily basis.

I am presently employed by Disabled People South Africa (DPSA) and am managing the Western Cape department. I have also recently been appointed as their National HIV/Aids Coordinator and am responsible for implementing HIV/Aids awareness-raising programmes in all the provinces. DPSA is a human rights organisation for persons with disabilities and the organisation, especially my boss, Mike Toni, has helped me to regain my confidence and taught me to believe in myself, despite my condition and the many times that I did not believe in myself.

I have come a long way. One of the things that helped me to come to terms with my condition is that I talk about it openly, hoping that this helps to break the stigma attached to it and also to dispel some of the myths attached to it.

I think that we need to change the perceptions of society to become more tolerant and accepting of disabled people.

It is society that disables us, not our disabilities.

Profile

Qualifications:
I obtained my matric at Luckoff High School and a BA degree in Social Work from the University of the Western Cape. I did Honours in Social Development at the University of Cape Town.

Occupation:
I am the Western Cape Provincial Development Co-ordinator for Disabled People South Africa. I serve on the Coordinating Committee for the Disability Studies Programme at UCT. I am also a volunteer counsellor for Rape Crisis.

Hobbies:
I enjoy working with people and assisting with their development.

Contact details:
email: hivaids@dpsa.gov.za
tel: 021 422 0357
cell: 082 416 9666

Gillian's Album

Me, in different stages of my life

« La tristesse m'a frappée seize mois plus tard [après la naissance de sa fille, ndlr] quand elle fut également diagnostiquée de méningite, la même maladie que j'avais eu enfant. [...] Au fil de mon parcours, j'ai vu nombre de discriminations contre les invalides. La société a une très faible considération à l'égard de l'handicap. »

Mariée, femme au foyer, mère de trois filles.
Elle fut la première sourde et mal voyante à obtenir l'examen d'entrée à l'université en Afrique du Sud.

Jonida Rahn

Deaf and visually impaired

I was born on 7 November 1945 on a farm called Maranda, in Villiersdorp. I was the second child of Danie and Martha le Roux. I was a normal baby.

At the age of five I contracted meningitis and was left a multi-disabled person. I have poor vision. I am deaf and I am physically disabled. Like most deaf people, my speech has been influenced, but my sense of smell has remained a hundred per cent.

At the age of seven I went to the De Villiers Graaff Primary school. I am very grateful for the three years I was able to attend a normal school as it was to my advantage later in life. My brother Pietie was such a great help. He meant so much to me in such a short space of time, especially during my first year at school and even the time following my disease. He taught me English, the alphabet and many rhymes and songs. He always ensured that I played along whenever there were other children around.

A normal school knows very little about how to teach the deaf or visually impaired, and only a few of the children and teachers could talk to me. At times they would write to me. To this day I prefer it if people write something. I was, however, fortunate enough to have a dear friend, Elsa. She cared about me and meant so much to me. She assisted me in everything I did in the classroom and always read me my marks after tests or exams. She also helped with my confirmation as a member of our church.

I then went to the School for the Deaf in Worcester, but I did not fit in. I could not read the quick sign language from a distance. So after six weeks, I went to the School for the Blind. I attended the section for the deaf-blind and there I fitted in very well. There were more people there who could talk to me. I was one of the first five students to attend this special section for deaf-blind students. I felt at home amongst people with the same disability that I have.

After completion of Grade 8, the school was not keen to register me for Grade 9, but I kept on pleading that I wanted to pass Grade 10. They gave me the opportunity to start with three subjects per year. I became the first deaf-blind person in South Africa to complete my junior certificate. After this achievement, I began to tackle the next one, matric, but I decided to stop after completing Grade 11.

I spent a few years working as a weaver at the Institute for the Blind and then I got married! Three beautiful daughters were born from this marriage. When I fell pregnant with my eldest child, Marlene, I felt exactly like a normal woman. My cup overflowed with joy. I had no problems during the pregnancy or during labour. I wasn't even scared that she would be disabled. When she was placed in my arms for the first time, it was an incredible feeling of elation and appreciation. The day I left the hospital the doctor asked me who was going to raise the child. I answered with confidence, 'I, myself!'

Sadness struck sixteen months later when she was also diagnosed with meningitis, the same illness I'd had as a child. It was such a shock. I prayed that she would not be as severally disabled as I am, but God decided otherwise. During her illness I kept on praying and God carried me through. He wanted us to be the same. Today I have a great understanding with this special child. We encourage each other and talk about normal people's approach to disabled people. We share jokes that normal people don't find funny.

After this first pregnancy, my cup overflowed again, and then again with my next two pregnancies. My other two daughters are both normal and just as precious to me. I really am blessed with my children and truly thankful to God. The fact that I have given birth to them and am able to raise them has been the biggest honour and blessing from above.

While I was in Kimberley at the Elizabeth School for the Physically Disabled, I used to take the train from Kimberley to Worcester. Usually there was a chaperone with us. During the long holidays, we were a large group. I developed a real love for travelling by train.

At the age of fifteen I took the challenge of travelling alone for a short holiday. I was the only girl with a bunch of boys from my school, but I didn't even know their names. The boys didn't bother me. I was excited to be alone in my own compartment. As the train left Kimberley station, a big bird flew from the branch of a tree and I could see it soaring up into the sky. At that moment I felt that I was also as free as a bird. Up to this day, I keep thinking of that moment.

During those years we travelled so much longer than we do today. We still had to travel around the pass, whereas today there is a tunnel between Worcester and Touws River. I thought it was the most beautiful scenery nature could offer. I never left my seat next to the window. Even when we passed this stretch after midnight, I would sneak out to stand by the window in the corridor.

God has provided me with a gift: He has placed a surprising number of anchors in my world. Some are not as stable as others, but at least they are friendly enough to fall with me. And there are always stable ones at the right places.

When I go out, I use my wheelchair as it is difficult to walk with someone. Furthermore, I read with the help of a magnifying glass. I read slowly, so I don't read that much anymore. My face has to be very close to the person who talks to me so that I can read their lips, and hear the sound of the words to ensure that I understand them. In general I can hear a few sounds and can distinguish between some, but there are so many sounds that my brain just can't identify. Because there are only a few people who understand me, and vice versa, I usually don't talk a lot. Except to those that I know can understand me.

When I think back on my life, there are only a few things I would have loved to do, one of them being to ride on a horse. We had a pony on the farm, but my parents refused to let me ride it. However, because I have a great faith in my Creator, and because I had the perfect parents who sacrificed a lot for me and always supported me and because I spent the greatest part of my life with other disabled people, I can accept my disability.

On my journey, I have seen a lot of discrimination against disabled people. Society has very little understanding of disability. Sometimes it really upsets me, but mostly I just laugh about it …

Profile

Qualifications:
I completed Grade 10 at the School for the Blind in Worcester.

Occupation:
I used to work at the Institue for the Blind. I became a housewife when my children were born.

Achievements:
I was the first deaf and visually impaired person to complete Grade 10 in South Africa.

Contact details:
email: nleroux@media24.com

Jonida & Marlene's album

Me as a young woman

My daughter Marlene in her school uniform.
Her profile is on page 68

You do not have to prove yourself just because you are a woman. And you most certainly do not have to prove yourself because of a disability. Some people are quite content to be just who they are. If you find yourself wondering why you don't have what it takes to do something different with your life, remember that most of us are driven by fear.

« Le recruteur m'a dit que j'étais une femme forte, intelligente mais que je ne convenais pas au poste parce que je serais incapable de faire face à la pression. [...] Je déteste quand les gens sont condescendants avec moi. [...] Ce sourire particulier plein de compassion, de pitié. C'est foudroyant pour la personne en face ».

Diplôme en Management financier.
Fondatrice et directrice éditoriale du magazine « We are Capable » pour les personnes invalides.
Élue Femme de l'année 2005, par le prix Shoprite /Checkers, dans le domaine des Arts et de la Culture.

You do not have to prove yourself just because you are a woman. And you most certainly do not have to prove yourself because of a disability. Some people are quite content to be just who they are. If you find yourself wondering why you don't have what it takes to do something different with your life, remember that most of us are driven by fear.

I am Julia Monoko Moloi, I am a 30 year-old businesswoman and the founder of the magazine, *We Are Capable*.

I was diagnosed with cerebral palsy as a baby, but my mother told me I was born this way. My granny and uncles told me I only turned this way at the age of two, but I don't care which story is true. Cerebral palsy strikes children in their first year of life and causes stiff muscles when you crawl or walk. It appears during the first few years of life and generally does not worsen over time.

My mother was faced with a very challenging situation. My father told her that I should be given up for adoption, because I wasn't like any other normal kid, but my mother knew that I was a gift from God and that I would be something one day. She taught me that God brought me here for a purpose.

I grew up in Ekurhuleni. My mother was working at Checkers, and the relationship between her and my late stepfather was very loving. They were my driving force. My family has always been the cornerstone of my life. I'm very proud of my mother.

Growing up, the other children would give me the eye because I was 'different'. I always responded by expressing my love for them. I think that's how life works. You've got to be strong and take the good with the bad as much as possible. I have come a long way to find my place and to make my mark. I have been exposed to the reality of life and that has made me strong.

There was a time when I felt ashamed of myself, because I was in two different environments at the same time. The first environment was living in a boarding school for people with disabilities, where I spent most of my life. The second one was when I had to go home and face people who were not disabled. I was still a teenager at the time and being in a school for the disabled made me realise that there was something wrong with my physical appearance.

I discovered the real me during the December of 1990. It was school holiday. While my friends were going out with their boyfriends, I was at home sleeping. My stepfather wanted me to go out and have fun with my boyfriend. He asked me why I was not with my boyfriend on that specific day. I asked him who would date a disabled person? He was very disappointed and angry by the way I responded. That's when he told me that I'm a beautiful, intelligent and energetic woman that any man would wish to have. He told me to walk tall and be proud of myself.

Three months after this conversation, I met a very handsome guy, who fell in love with me and accepted me for who I am. His friends wanted to know why he was dating a disabled woman. But he was never ashamed; instead, he was very proud of me. He used to encourage and motivate me to walk tall. He even helped me with my studies and I respect him to this day.

I attended a school for the disabled from 1982 to 1991 and then I changed to a mainstream school, St Mary's college, where children with disabilities were in the overwhelming minority. I managed to make good use of my sparkling personality to fit in and nobody discriminated against me.

In 1993 I completed my matric at Lee Rand High School. My goal here was to communicate with the teachers on behalf of other students and they would each pay me R5 for this service. The teachers were not aware of this, but it made me realise that I was quite intelligent.

I had a dream of becoming a chartered accountant. To quench my permanent yearning for accounting, when I finished school, I enrolled at the Germiston Technical College. That's where I graduated with a financial management diploma. I received a bursary and was ready to further my studies at university, but I got bitten by a bug of a different kind.

When you go out looking for a job, the first thing employers look at is your disability, rather than your capability.

I remember the day I was called for an interview. The interview went very well. The interviewer told me that I was a strong, intelligent woman, but that I was not suitable for the job because I wouldn't be able to cope with the pressure.

When we come across people with disabilities most of us are quick to call them 'cripples' and then look the other way. We refuse to face them because their condition questions and challenges our sense of responsibility and charity. As a matter of fact, I hate it when people *ag shame* me. People, mostly women, flash smiles at me. Not the kind of smiles most men would hope for from a woman, nor the neutral courtesy smile exchanged by strangers passing on the sidewalk, but that particular precious smile that mixes compassion, condescension and pity. It's withering to the person on the receiving end.

I hate it when people with disabilities don't do anything for themselves and resort to begging on the street. Charity and disability grants actually make them worse because everyone needs to contribute to their own support and to society in some way.

The problem has always been that society helps people with their disability rather than their ability.

Think about it. There are far more things everyone can do than things they can't do. Anyone who dwells on the things they can't do is disabled in their thinking. God designed us to be who we are through the empowerment of His spirit and to become successful and influential in our unique and different ways, be it at work or at home.

Something quite miraculous happened in 2005. It was the feather in my cap. I won the Woman of the Year Award in the Arts, Culture and Communications category. The Cape Town Convention Centre erupted into a wild applause when my name was called. As I walked towards the stage I felt ravishing in my black Jean Paul Gaultier evening gown.

Minister of Arts and Culture, Pallo Jordan, welcomed me to the microphone and I knelt down and cried, because people with disabilities are so seldom given a chance to prove themselves.

After thanking God I had to be honest and acknowledged that I didn't believe I was going to win the award because I was nominated with very powerful women.

'This is a rainbow nation,' I said, 'and we should work together. There should be acceptance, understanding and mutual respect. My way forward is to fight and raise awareness about issues that concern people with disabilities. I am fighting that musicians with disabilities should be invited or given a fair chance to perform in all festivals that are held in South Africa.'

Profile

Qualifications:
I matriculated at Lee Rand High School and obtained a Financial Management diploma from Germiston Technical College.

Occupation:
I am the founder and editorial director of *We Are Capable*, a magazine for people with disabilities.

Achievements:
I won the Shoprite/Checkers Woman of the Year Award in 2005 (Arts and Culture category).

Contact details:
email: julia@wearecapable.co.za
cell: 082 391 1440
tel: 011 916 1526

Julia's album

Photos of a younger me

I am a passionate, energetic, successful and beautiful woman with a disability.
I am not a disabled woman.

Karen Smit

Juvenile chronic arthritis

« Quand arrêteront-ils de m'enfoncer des aiguilles et de me nourrir de pilules et de médicaments ? [...] C'est dur d'accepter que notre sensualité soit toujours perçue de manière superficielle. L'apparence physique conditionne tout... »

Mariée, une fille.
Master en Travail Social Industriel (Université de Stellenbosh).
En cours d'acquisition d'un doctorat en Management du Changement à Vodacom.
Consultante spécialisée des emplois pour les personnes invalides.

I realise now that as a teenager and later as a young woman with a disability, I locked my sensuality away.

It was all in accordance with the opinions and unwritten laws of an able society, where being different meant being less.

I was three years old when I was diagnosed with juvenile chronic arthritis. Initially my thoughts were limited to my reaction to many painful hospital visits: 'This physiotherapy is so painful. I wish it would stop, but I have to go through with it …'; 'I haven't seen my family for months. When can I go home again?'; 'When will they stop pushing needles into me and stop feeding me tablets and medicines?' (To this day I dislike taking tablets), and 'After this treatment I should be able to walk again and use my hands.'

I grew up in a small seaside town. In general, prejudice and negative attitudes towards disabled people seem to be worse in small towns, possibly because everyone knows everybody else's business. So besides my physical struggle, I have also internalised the unwritten words, thoughts and rules of society in terms of being disabled and a woman. These myths state that because you are disabled you may not be or feel sensual, beautiful or sexy. It is a sad truth that sensuality is perceived in the shallowest of terms: your physical appearance is everything. Being a young woman with a disabled body meant that no guy could possibly ever be interested in me and of course I believed these lies wholeheartedly.

As a teenager my emotions were often conflicted: I struggled to understand why I sometimes felt beautiful and even sexy, when the world around me kept telling me that I couldn't. I enjoyed going out with my friends, but as soon as it seemed that a guy might be interested in me, I acted as if I was not interested, because I had been brainwashed into believing that I was not desirable. This, in spite of the fact that quite a number of guys were interested in dating me. If only I knew then what I know now.

Although I was quite reserved when it came to establishing relationships with the opposite sex, I really wanted a boyfriend just like all my girlfriends. Instead I would end up just watching my friends, following their relationships as they started, flourished and ended. My girlfriends would usually confide in me and would share endless relationship issues and I listened patiently and empathised with them. As a friend and a disabled one at that, I could not possibly be a threat to their relationship, so I was always cast in the role of the intimate advisor. And so I lived through their relationships, secretly dreaming and wishing that one day I too would have someone who would love and want me.

The idea of me getting a man and getting married was an issue that everyone avoided, because the answer was (in their minds at least) so painfully obvious. And every night I prayed that it would happen to me. I kept this wish secret – not sharing it with even my closest friends or family members. This was because if men were interested in me, they would just fall for me because they felt sorry for me. They would then use me and dump me after a couple of months, because I would be a burden and would not be able to contribute to the household.

In my mid-twenties I realised that if I stayed at home, I would seal my own fate. So, in spite of many protestations and a full doomsday brigade (my family had the habit of hurting me with kindness), I moved to Cape Town to live and work on my own. At the age of 29, I decided to go to university to study for a degree. Again the naysayers tore their clothes and threw ash over their heads.

In Stellenbosch I lived in a house with three male students and we had a great time. Through the open-minded attitudes of the young people who surrounded me, I finally went through a somewhat reckless adolescence.

Those three years did wonders for my self-confidence and my sense of self-worth soared, no longer imprisoned by my alternatively abled physicality.

Crunch-time came when I met the man who would eventually become my husband. To my complete disbelief he saw me as a beautiful young woman and could not stand being away from me. This was my first true experience of falling in love. He not only accepted me, but did so with unconditional love. For the first time someone saw me. Karen. A woman worth loving just because of who she was. Not because she was an object of pity. It took a while for me to accept that he loved me for who I was.

Paul's enveloping love for me healed so many areas of my life that I started allowing myself to openly feel beautiful and sensual. He believed that I was gorgeous; now I had to believe the same thing, and bit by surprising bit, it happened.

My husband and I got married when I was 30. For the first time the doomsday brigade was quiet. I realised that they were just trying to protect me and tears of joy flowed at our wedding. But some people still wondered why this fully abled man was interested in marrying me. This question led to others: What if he gets tired of assisting me? What if I am a financial burden and am not able to hold onto a job? What if I need to have more surgery?

Today we have been married for 13 years and I am proud to say that our relationship is so strong that we have been able to overcome each and every challenge that came our way.

At the age of 39 I fell pregnant and our daughter Kelly was born in September 2002. Getting the positive test results from my doctor was the most amazing moment in my life and one I will always remember. I treasured each day that I carried Kelly, talking to her and feeling tremendously proud that I would soon be a mom. Her birth was a miracle as I had to undergo an emergency Caesarean and she was born prematurely at 28 weeks. We both pulled through and I am glad to say that we are both fine and that she is the most beautiful girl I have ever seen. In the beginning being pregnant was completely overwhelming for me – I realised this when my brother and I went to shop for a christening outfit for my unborn child. At that stage I was not yet visibly pregnant and the sales lady asked me who this outfit was for. The moment was just too big for me and I found it hard to say out loud, The outfit is for my daughter, so I kept quiet until my brother came to my rescue. From that point onwards I used the word as often as I could. I was going to have a daughter.

Ever since childhood I have dreamt of just being an ordinary woman. I did not want to be pitied and I did not really see myself as being different although I was quite aware that there were certain things that I was not able to do. However, I could do most things and somehow, despite sometimes overwhelming odds, I kept on believing and hoping that one day I would also be able to live a 'normal' life. From a very young age I had to fight against the reality that people wanted to create for me:

Your disability is the reason for your parents' divorce.
(My parents were the reason for their divorce.)
You will not become older than 13.
(As I write this I have just turned 43.)
Completing matric has no use for you.
(Well, it gave me the right to study.)
You cannot move out of the town where you were born.
(I have been in Cape Town for 17 years.)
You will not be able to study further.
(I have just started my Ph.D.)
You will end up in a home, where people will take care of you.
(I have my own fabulous home, thank you.)
You will never get a job.
(I fill a crucial post for a multinational firm and I have my own consulting business.)
You will never be able to drive a car.
(I have to admit, I do tend to speed.)
No man will ever love you.
(Let me introduce you to my gorgeous husband, Paul.)
You will never have a child.
(Kelly. My daughter's name is Kelly, meaning 'fighter'. Just like her mother.)

Of course I feel despondent at times, but I always guard against adopting a 'victim' attitude. I always manage to lift my head and believe that I can do anything if I put my mind to it and just keep pushing forward. The more successful I become, the more it motivates me to keep going to achieve my dreams and goals. My journey of adversity has caused me to become tenacious, resilient, and optimistic: all invaluable allies in overcoming obstacles.

I have learnt to accept myself and by doing so I have started to celebrate life by living each day with a positive attitude. I am not a super-human being and also believe that God has not given me special favours because I happen to have a disability. I have realised that my inviting personality and my positive attitude supersede my physical disability. Ultimately it is my will, attitude, passion and perseverance that determine to what extent I live my life successfully. And those qualities override any disability.

I am a passionate, energetic, successful and beautiful woman with a disability. I am not a disabled woman.

Profile

Qualifications:
I matriculated at Point High School (my friends carried my school case and the rugby team carried me up the stairs – the school was three storeys high). I received a master's degree in Industrial Social Work from the University of Stellenbosch and am currently busy with my Ph.D.

Occupation:
I am a Senior Transformation Specialist at Vodacom and I have my own consulting business specialising in disability employment.

Hobbies:
Taking train trips, music, shows, theatre and socialising with friends.

Contact details:
email: karensmit50@gmail.com
tel: 011 653 5724

You will not become older than 13.
(As I write this I have just turned 43.)
Completing matric has no use for you.
(Well, it gave me the right to study.)
You cannot move out of the town where you were born.
(I have been in Cape Town for 17 years.)
You will not be able to study further.
(I have just started my Ph.D.)
You will end up in a home, where people will take care of you.
(I have my own fabulous home, thank you.)
You will never get a job.
(I fill a crucial post for a multinational firm and I have my own consulting business.)
You will never be able to drive a car.
(I have to admit, I do tend to speed.)
No man will ever love you.
(Let me introduce you to my gorgeous husband, Paul.)
You will never have a child.
(Kelly. My daughter's name is Kelly, meaning 'fighter'. Just like her mother.)

Karen's album

ust before contracting the disease

In my younger days ...

My wedding day

With my husband and Kelly

Holding beautiful Kelly

« En raison des opérations à répétition, je suis restée à l'hôpital les cinq premières années de ma vie. Je voyais les docteurs et les aides soignantes comme s'ils avaient été ma propre famille. Alors, quand ma mère m'a dit : 'Maggie, on rentre à la maison', je n'ai pas répondu parce que je ne comprenais pas ce que signifiait le mot 'maison' ».

Médailles d'or et d'argent en dance de salon avec fauteuil roulant.
Membre de comité de sports locaux indépendants œuvrant pour améliorer les évènements réservés aux personnes invalides et attirer de nouveaux membres.

Magdalene *Leepi*

Paraplegic

My name is Magdalene Leepi and I was born on 17 January 1963. At birth I was diagnosed with clubfeet and was classified as a walking paraplegic. Due to constant operations, I remained in hospital for the first five years of my life. I considered the doctors and nurses to be my family. So when my mom said: 'Maggie, I'm taking you home!' I didn't reply because I didn't know what the word 'home' meant. I was nervous because I didn't know what would be expected of me once I reached this place called 'home'. At the age of six, I was finally sent home and for the first time I saw faces I had never seen before. My family.

I soon realised that being 'home' wasn't as bad as I thought it would be. My parents treated me just like they did my older sister, Marlyn. Normal was the norm. In other words, I had a very normal upbringing. Being disabled didn't mean I was exempt from discipline.

My parents never saw me as a disabled person, and it has made me who I am today: a normal woman with normal hobbies like candle-wicking, making potplant holders, découpage, cooking, reading romance novels, dancing, travelling, meeting new people and arranging flowers.

My parents also thought it necessary to enrol me in a normal primary school. My mom demanded the teachers treat me as they would any of the other children. However, the teachers were sceptical anyway and treated me with kid gloves, but they soon realised that I could be just as naughty, or maybe even worse. My very first school report shows evidence of my unruly behaviour at school. My first grade teacher said: 'Maggie is a problem child!' My classmates, on the other hand, accepted me as they would have any other normal person.

I went through all the stages children go through, with exactly the same joy and turmoil. It wasn't long before I experienced puppy love. A boy named Christopher had a crush on me and he seemed to be the most charming and funniest boy ever. This crush lasted for a whole year after which we were separated by being put into different classes. And then, there was a boy named Irwin who left me for somebody else and I was devastated because I felt I wasn't pretty enough. At 12, I started developing breasts and I became very conscious of my body. When my menstruation cycle began, my mom seriously warned me to stay away from boys. This puzzled me, but I didn't adhere to her warnings. Other teenage feelings such as worthlessness soon surfaced. It felt like my world had ended and I was angry at myself for falling in love. I soon realised that the saying 'time heals all wounds' was very true. I started to feel confident and comfortable in my body again. My breasts were my best asset and I liked wearing tight-fitting tops to accentuate them. I was really turning into a beautiful woman. I believe … *if you have it, flaunt it!*

During my final year at primary school a sister came to our school to inject us with what I think was a polio vaccination. She questioned me about what school I would go to the following year. I told her that I was planning to stay at home because I felt I wouldn't be able to cope at a normal high school. At primary school level we remained in one class and the teachers rotated from class to class, but in high school I would have to move around between classes. I told her I wasn't sure about whether I'd be able to cope in that type of environment because my experience with normal, older children was that they became very intolerant of kids who needed assistance in carrying books.

She came to our home and told my parents about Astra School for the Physically Disabled. They thought it was a good idea to send me there and once again I became exposed to an environment that was totally foreign to me. Suddenly I was amongst people who looked like me. Even though I didn't feel comfortable with the idea of being amongst disabled people, I managed to make lifelong friends. I stayed at this school for three years, but I wasn't stimulated enough with regards to education. The school concentrated mainly on the physical needs of the pupils, so I started motivating and educating myself by reading as much as I could.

I became very interested in building my upper body strength, and after I left Astra, I did some research on the gymnasiums in my area. I found none of them to be suitable for disabled people. Stairs were always a major obstacle as well as equipment that were not suited for disabled bodies. Eventually I heard about Protea Sports Club for the disabled and joined. This was my light at the end of the tunnel. Shotput, javelin and discus became my forte for several years after that. I was, however, dissatisfied with the effect it had on the shape of my body. My upper arms became huge and my breasts became smaller. I felt I needed to do something sporty, but perhaps a bit more ladylike.

My prayers were answered, because soon afterwards I heard about wheelchair ballroom. It sounded like a refreshingly graceful challenge so I enrolled in a dance school which specialised in teaching wheelchair ballroom. My dream to strut my stuff finally came true. My dance instructor was extremely patient and caring towards all of her students because she was able to adapt to a disabled person's way of dancing in a wheelchair.

Initially we danced with old, heavy and rusted chairs, but I didn't care because I had the most fun ever. We learnt to dance with able-bodied as well as disabled individuals. I enjoyed dancing with the able-bodied persons the most, because it gave me the freedom to express myself. I also loved the physical workout. We practised at St Giles Sports Club in Rondebosch every Friday and I would wait anxiously for that day to arrive every week.

After a year of dancing with the old chairs, the Lotto sponsored about eight brand new chairs, which were specially made for dancing. I felt like a butterfly on the floor with my new light-weight wheelchair.

My big chance to really show off came when I was selected for the Western Province team. I was ecstatic, to say the least, and I could hardly wait to get home to tell my family the good news.

My first competition took place in Johannesburg. I was so nervous, but also very confident. I didn't win any medals, but the experience was phenomenal and it gave me emotional strength.

A year after this competition I got a new dancing partner. He was tall and slender and reminded me of Fred Astaire. We became like one person when we were on the dance floor and every movement flowed naturally. The time came for me to enter another competition. This time I won a trophy with my able-bodied partner for the best dressed couple. I also won a silver medal for Latin. And when the gold medal winner's number was announced, I didn't know whether I should laugh or cry. Instead, I froze. My partner had to nudge me to bring me out of my shocked daze so that I could accept my medal. A gold medal for Ballroom with my disabled partner. I was really starting to enjoy life. Emotions were high and I was proud to be a member of the Western Province team!

As a student and competitor of this school, I managed to go places I never dreamt possible. We danced anywhere we were asked to: in theatres, for old people in homes, at anniversary celebrations, birthday parties and church functions. Dancing has helped me to overcome my shyness. Now I simply thrive in the spotlight!

Presently, I have taken a temporary break from dancing to dedicate some time to try to improve sport for the disabled at my local sports club. I serve on the club committee and I'm concentrating on recruiting new members to do field events. I would also like to pursue coaching field events.

Profile

Qualifications:
I completed my Grade 8.

Occupation:
I was a contract worker at APD for three years. I worked at URO Laize International on a full-time basis for one year and six months until the company went bankrupt.

Hobbies:
Ballroom dancing: the adrenaline rush before a ballroom competition gets me very excited, because I know there are people in the audience who expect me to do well.

Contact details:
tel: 021 712 7782
cell: 083 372 9647

My dancing made the papers

GESTREMDHEID KRY HUL NIE ONDER

Dansers met gestremdhede wys hul staal by die opening van die Wes-Kaapse Spesiale Olimpiese Spele. Die openingseremonie is by die rekreasiesentrum in Bellville-Suid gehou. Berig, foto binne.

Magdalene's album

Photos throughout my life

Many people that are deaf and blind lead very quiet lives, even though their minds are yearning for more attention, more opportunities, wisdom, knowledge, more friends, more acceptance and more awareness.

« Nous étions à Windhoek pour les vacances quand je suis tombée malade. J'ai été soignée trop tard. Je suis devenue sourde, mal voyante et invalide. […] J'avais peu d'amis. […] Je suis tombée amoureuse de quelques garçons. Ça ne durait jamais longtemps. Aujourd'hui, je regarde en arrière et je me dis que la plupart du temps c'était surtout de l'amitié ».

Une parmi trois sœurs.
Assistante de stérilisation des équipements pour théâtre, à la Medi-clinic.

Marlene Rahn

Deaf and visually impaired

I was born normal. I contracted meningitis when I was only sixteen months old. We were in Windhoek on holiday when I got sick. I was treated too late. I was left deaf, visually impaired and physically disabled.

Because I was so little, I accepted my disability rather easily. A toddler doesn't really realise what is going on. When I realised it later on, it was already such a part of my life.

There are times when I wish I could hear better. It is very difficult to be this way. Many people that are deaf and blind lead very quiet lives, even though their minds are yearning for more attention, more opportunities, wisdom, knowledge, more friends, more acceptance and more awareness.

My parents treated me very well. They gave me a lot of attention and tried to raise me as 'normal' as they could. Obviously I couldn't do everything normal kids could do, but I did play outside a lot and climbed trees with the neighbourhood children. We rode around on our tricycles and I was actually quite naughty.

My parents did a lot for me. My father carried me around a lot as a toddler. At the age of twelve, they made me a tricycle. My father helped me a great deal with improving my speech. They also organised Sunday school lessons for me and ensured that I was confirmed as a proper member of the church. They made sure that I learnt English at school.

My tricycle remains a good form of transport to this day. I approach challenges with it, like buying groceries.

I have very few friends. Some of my best friends were at school with me.

Things have changed as I get older. I keep myself busy. I read a lot, chat a lot and write to penpals, and I make myself lovely sweets.

There have been some guys I fell for. None of it ever really lasted long. Today I look back and think it was mostly always only friendship and that the guys were just being friendly.

Through all these years I've had a longing for a lifelong friend, but I have to accept things as they are.

My motto has always been to do what you don't think you can. I have achieved a lot. I have even taught myself how to use a cellphone.

There are a lot of things I want to do. I want to finish matric, but it is very difficult to get the help I need.

I actually want a husband who will join me and be an activist. Someone who will help me to open other people's eyes. And to open doors for me that are always closed.

My Creator leads me where He wants me.

Profile

Qualifications:
I completed Grade 8.

Occupation:
I am an assistant in sterilising theatre equipment at Medi-Clinic. I enjoy working with normal people.

Hobbies:
I enjoy playing chess and reading. I also attend computer lessons every weekend.

Contact details:
sms to: 072 838 1240
email: marlener79@gmail.com

Note: You can see my photo in my mom's album on page 51.

It's not their disabilities that set these women apart

It's their absolute refusal to accept limitations of any kind. At Absa, nothing inspires us more than seeing an obstacle being turned into an opportunity. Which is why we're dedicated to helping organisations like Casual Day raise awareness of, and empower people with disabilities. After all, the measure of success lies not in the achievement itself but in what was overcome to achieve it.

ABSA

Today, tomorrow, together.

« Le docteur leur a dit : 'Qu'est ce que vous en savez, vous ? Vous ne voyez pas que ce sont simplement ses dents qui lui font mal ?' Et au cours du week-end, j'ai contracté la polio. [...] Une fille estropiée n'aurait pas été présentable sur scène. Alors, on m'a demandé de rester dans les coulisses et de chanter pour renforcer la voix du soliste sur scène. »

Mariée, deux enfants.
Master en Musicologie puis en Éducation à l'Université de Western Cape.
Doctorat en management à l'université de Stellenbosh.
Ancienne directrice, présidente et membre des conseils d'administration de nombreuses organisations.
Membre de la commission CRL et lauréate de plusieurs Prix d'Honneur.
Directrice du département Développement des publics et Éducation à Artscape.

I was born in Wellington, a scenic little town surrounded by mountains. My mother, Christine le Roux, was married for only three months when she realised she had made a terrible mistake. Off she rushed, back to her parents and nine other siblings. To top this, I announced my intention to become one of my granny's many children. Yes, in total we were eleven children. Naturally, my granny became 'Ma' and my maternal mother became 'Tittie' (big sister).

The culture of our family was extremely conservative and religious, and to my grandparents, Tittie's divorce was a scandal. My grandmother's maiden name was Abrahams, and to their minds, the Abrahams family was a cut above the other coloureds in their street. Ironically, we lived in Versailles Street, which was a very fancy French address for a family who lived from hand to mouth in the *skema*, which was nothing more than the council's housing systems. Although we were dirt poor, Ma (my granny) being a domestic worker and a seasonal fruit picker on the surrounding farms, had a good reputation as a fine Christian woman. She liked to remind us that her dad was a white Englishman.

Pa, on the other hand, was always fighting with the 'boere' (the white Afrikaners) about his rights as a cleaner in the local factory, the Western Tannery. He was such an intelligent man and the only person in our street who could read and write English, so he never felt inferior to the 'boere'. This very often cost him his job.

It was to this scenario that my mother returned, pregnant, to share a room with her two sisters and her granny. And with Ma's tenth child who was only one year old. The family then started to live off Tittie's unemployment fund and later on her maternity leave income. She was an extremely beautiful and talented singer, but life was harsh for her. She needed to survive on behalf of all of us, who depended on her income.

On 17 September 1967 I arrived with blonde hair, and a fair skin. I can just imagine Ma's joy that I looked so white; everything that she aspired to. Tittie then decided that my name should be Marlene. My journey started as Marlene le Roux. Yes, so French, and living in Versailles Street in a very divided community, at the heart of apartheid.

When I fell ill one Friday, my aunt Marjorie and Tittie took me to the white doctor, in the scrunching heat (Wellington is known to reach temperatures of up to 40 degrees). They walked with the sick child in the unbearable heat, only to be reprimanded by an insensitive doctor who they had to argue with – as he was not giving me the proper attention they had hoped for. Apparently he then told them: 'What do you people know. Can't you see she is teething?' And over that weekend I contracted polio.

For my family, the world had collapsed. The white, blonde, little girl whom they so fondly and with such pride showed off to people, was not perfect anymore. The community even accused my mother of being cursed because of her divorce.

Tittie's beauty was frowned upon by women, but the men were intrigued. Mothers would warn their sons against her. In a deprived community like ours, strong-willed women were not tolerated. But for Tittie and Ma these were side factors. For them, I became priority.

All their lives they had fought for survival; now the road had only a few more obstacles.

Their first encounter with the Red Cross was a humiliation. After getting up at four o'clock in the morning, walking for an hour to the station and enduring many hours on the train with another long distance to walk, they were treated like illiterate, rural coloured women who ought to have known that they should have gone to the clinic for vaccination. Guilt started to be reinforced.

Nevertheless, I was flourishing in a house that only gave me un-conditional love, though subtly made it clear that I was different. My first steps were with an ugly calliper. And I remember my stylish mother, Tittie, as she mourned: 'Oh what is going to happen to my little girl!' And Ma being stern: 'You must have faith in the Lord, Christiegirl!'

Despite all challenges, we are a jovial lot. Tittie loved to sing and I used to join her. Before long I was entertaining family and friends with my songs. Tittie started to realise that I was gifted. I had a singing talent and that gave me a sense of control and achievement.

I realised that not only could I compete with normal people, but I could do better than them.

Tittie was now even more proud of me. She would get extremely upset when people said: 'Ag shame, man. Look at the beautiful little cripple.' They used to put money in my hand. Even the poorest of the poor farm workers. This annoyed Tittie endlessly. She would react with: 'I have my pride!'

What softened my plight was the fact that people thought I was pretty, and I assume it all was because of the fair skin. But then there were those who would make callous remarks about my crippled leg or speculate that I was mature before my time and that nothing would become of me. Thus the seed was sowed to breed my insecurity. I became intensely aware that I was different in a community that did not tolerate imperfections. Once Tittie took me to a charismatic church leader, who was supposed to pray for me and heal me. It did not happen, and he told me over and over that it was my fault as my faith had not been strong enough. I carried the scars of this for many years. My saving grace was the fact that I could never let Tittie down, even if I had to pretend to everybody. I was her pride and joy and had to reassure her over and over again that it was okay that I had this crippled leg; that I was fine with it. Then she would always ponder whether the boys would be interested in me.

My first day at school was traumatic. Tittie made it clear that I was intelligent and that I did not need special treatment. She made sure that the teacher understood this, but the message was also loud and clear that if anything went wrong, she would personally deal with the teacher. To this day I am still amazed when I try to figure out how she managed to pay for a taxi to take me to school every day.

All I wanted to do was to make Tittie and Ma proud. At primary school my talent was reinforced when I won medal after medal for singing. I became the child with the amazingly mature singing voice. I toured the entire Boland area singing at farms, school concerts and church halls. On stage I became myself without the crippled leg. I liked the admiration of people and it gave me that sense of normality. I will never forget one specific evening at a church gathering on one of the farms, Blou Vlei. After I had sung 'Yes, Jesus loves me', this extremely poor community threw their last money on the stage to show their appreciation.

My primary-school years were wonderful, even though half of the time was spent at the Princess Alice home. I had so many operations and always had to cope with a mother who had to go back to Wellington. I used to cry my heart out. But my singing made up for this. I actively participated in the school and church choirs and sang my heart out. Once my world nearly came to a standstill when the church produced an operetta, and even though I was the choir's soloist, the producer did not choose me to sing the lead. What added to my pain and astonishment was that I overheard him saying: 'A crippled girl would not look good on stage.' I was asked to stay behind the stage and sing to strengthen the projection of the lead singer. My mother was furious. She threatened to take me out of the choir, but I pleaded because I wanted to be part of the production. I tried to convince her that I was okay, but at night it haunted me. I made a vow to myself that nothing would ever break my spirit. On the whole, everything in my life remained in a delicate balance where sadness was always followed by gladness. After the operetta incident, my music teacher entered me for the Eisteddfod in Cape Town and I won a gold medal …

I was only ten years old when I became attracted to boys. But they were only interested in my singing. As I grew older it became even worse, for the boys would only see me as a very good friend in whom they could confide, and needless to say, none of the girls saw me as a threat. During these turbulent times, my best friend Marion also wore two callipers and walked with crutches. We had a little private game where we would sit down somewhere so that our callipers were out of sight and then we would flirt with all the boys passing by. Then just as they made a move and sat down with us, one of us would get up and go to the toilet just to see how their facial expressions changed into utmost disgust and extreme disappointment.

I became a very good listener and decided to concentrate on my school work and my music. I knew I had natural rhythm, but the irony was that even though I was every boy's best friend, no one would ever ask me to go to the local disco. I experienced the awkwardness of these boys during my puberty as extremely painful. So I started to concentrate on my girlfriends, who eventually became my pillars of strength. My three friends Caureen, Johleen and Lexy shared their love stories with me and through them I started my own journey into womanhood. They took me with them to parties and clubs and taught me to dance. They were important links in building my confidence. They would, for instance, always tell me how beautiful and sexy my one leg was. With my newly acquired confidence, I became a keen swimmer. In the water I was so normal and I noticed that the boys admired me. I also enjoyed that I was a better swimmer than most of them, and I would stay in the water as long as possible because I knew that once out of the water, rejection would follow.

Strange how older men always looked at me differently. One incident still stays with me. Wellington is renowned for its Klopse carnival, and my cousins and I used to follow the dancing carnivals through the streets. On one such an occasion one of the Klopse men looked at me and suddenly groped one of my breasts and proclaimed: 'You have beautiful breasts!' I should have been shocked, but what amazed me was that it felt so good. I could see the lust in his eyes and it made me feel powerful. The procession moved on and he will never know what that act of sexual harassment meant to me.

During high school I was quite mature in handling my attraction towards the opposite sex, even though my body was yearning for physical touch. Rules of the mating game prescribed that the first step should be left to the man to initiate, but I knew this would not work for me. I needed to make the first move. Instinctively, I took matters into my own hands to ensure the experience of a first kiss.

One night in my wonderful, supportive neighbourhood, I met this boy who praised my singing, and under the lamppost I initiated my first kiss, in full view of the whole neighbourhood. Suddenly they saw me in a different light. No more Marlenetjie for me. Oh, how I liked the wetness of his lips. I often reflect upon my strict Calvinistic upbringing, and then I regret that golden rule of no sex before marriage . . . I could have been so experienced!

I was the first woman in my immediate family who was accepted to go to university. My mother was over the moon, but so worried about the money for my studies! With my school years drawing to a close, I dreamt of the opera stage and applied at the University of Cape Town. Unfortunately they turned me down with the excuse that there was no place for disability on stage. Eventually I ended up at the University of the Western Cape. What a liberating and life-changing experience it was! Politics, danger, mystery, fearlessness and for the first time ever, being away from Tittie and Ma. For the first time in my life I was sleeping alone on a bed, not sharing it with two other persons.

The real awakening of Marlene le Roux happened on the back of a truck of student activists. We were on our way to Crossroads, a black township near Phillipi. A group of black vigilantes, namely the Witdoeke, had been hired by the apartheid boere (what we called the police in those days). Their mission was to fight black activists, create division and to kill our comrades. Our mission was to assist the women and children who were seeking refuge in a nearby church. In the truck on this dangerous mission, out of the blue, two comrades were suddenly both interested in me. My first flirtation with womanhood started. There they were, both trying to be first in helping me off the truck and commenting on how beautiful I was! At first I was sceptical, but then I started to enjoy the attention. So afraid of rejection, however, I bluntly asked one of them: 'Do you notice that I am disabled? My friend is the beautiful one.' He laughed as if I was being silly and said: 'Who cares!' He wanted to take me to his parent's shack nearby. Maybe it was the danger, the burning shacks, the little ones running around with Vaseline. But when the boere teargassed the church, everyone fled and in the midst of it all, I became fearless and said yes to the comrade. Walking through burning shacks, I forgot that I was a cripple. Lying on a double bed, in his parent's shack, I also forgot that I was a cripple. All that I could think of was being in the arms of this comrade and feeling completely loved. No, we did not have sex – at that stage my strict upbringing would not allow me to give myself completely to this young man – but he became so hard just touching me, and what an awakening that was. The compliment: that I could have this effect on someone, and all this while the flames were raging outside … We were just in time to catch the truck back to campus, everybody looking at me, frowning, wondering . . .

This experience gave me the courage to flirt. I was fully conscious of the power a woman has over a man. I still had my insecurities, the little voice whispering: careful, don't give too much, remember the rejection. I developed a fool-proof strategy in my relationship with men: I would always get involved with men who were unavailable; men with girl-friends, who were interested in me, but whom I knew would not leave their girlfriends. In a weird way, I found security in having no expectations. I never had serious commitments, so I could be on my own stage, always the happy one, but on the inside my heart was broken.

At one stage I decided to take up ballroom. Not even the instructor's remark that he could not teach a disabled person put me off at all. I told

him I would show him, and then waltzed perfectly. I never gave up; I was always proving myself, searching for something. I thought nothing of joining an all-male gospel group. As the only female, I drew a lot of attention from the men in the group and from all the audiences. This gave me that final boost I was searching for, to be on stage again and receive the sense of acceptance and admiration from society. I was a new person, fully aware of my sensuality. I knew which parts of my body I liked, and what clothes to wear to accentuate these. I liked teeny- weeny short dresses, and did not care what people thought of my calliper: it has now become my stilettos, my Dior bag.

I turned my calliper and ugly shoes into my very personal trademark. I did not need the affirmation of a lover any more. I rediscovered my laughter, and used it mostly to laugh at myself.

Men found this attitude so irresistible that I was now in a position where I could send men away from me – all those that I was not interested in.

And then out of the blue a man came along. One that did not know that I could sing, did not know my history, one that made me feel that it was okay just to be me. I felt safe and so loved in his company. I fell deeply in love with this man who was only mine. My body woke up from a long sleep; being loved made me more aware of myself. Again, I changed my dress style. My breasts became more beautiful to me and my most precious asset was my right leg. I started to accentuate it more.

I needed the security so I asked him to marry me. Oh, Tittie and Ma could not understand that I wanted to get married! Ma asked him several times whether he was sure that he wanted to marry me. She kept on reminding him that I had polio and that my health was not a hundred per cent. Tittie just became distant; she said very little. I think she really did her fair share of mourning when I left for university. As for myself, I needed to be able to say to people that I was married. To say: 'This here is my husband! ' And I was already dreaming of children …

Six months into the marriage, a doctor discovered a brain tumour. I survived the operation, but left the hospital with the shocking news that I would never have children. For days I could not concentrate. People around me would rejoice in the fact that I had survived the operation. 'It is a miracle!' they said, but I felt like a failure. Eventually I told myself: 'You will survive this as well. This too shall pass.'

Five years later, I fell pregnant with my daughter Aimee. Oh, did I enjoy this pregnancy! It was an experience beyond all expectations, and at the time of our country's first local elections to boot. Being pregnant gave me enormous energy; motherhood was just what I wanted.

After the birth of my daughter, it did not take long for the old sense of unworthiness to appear again. I had to be reassured of my worth. I needed a second child, a boy this time. I would teach him how to be sensitive to women and to appreciate them. I was overjoyed when I discovered I was pregnant again, and even more so when it was confirmed that it was indeed a boy. I wanted to shout to the world: 'Look at me! I have done it again.' I could see the admiration in the eyes of people. This was nine months of bliss and a wonderful feeling of sensuality for me. I was so happy.

A month before my son's birth I read the book *Expecting Adam,* and I had an instant connection with the author and the main character. I never contemplated then that this would be the beginning of the most challenging journey of my life. My beautiful boy was born absolutely normal. Adam of the book has never left me, and the minute I laid my eyes on my son, he became my Adam.

When Adam developed a fever on his second day, nothing could reassure me; I knew he was different. For six months we visited the paediatricians on a weekly basis. Time and again they told us that everything was fine. We spent a small fortune on every remedy we heard of, just to get the child to stop crying. Then we changed paediatricians and my worst nightmare was confirmed. I became the parent of a disabled child.

So what does one do when your reality becomes what society defines as 'not normal'?

I believe the first step is to face the world through your own eyes and not through the confirmation of others. Affirming yourself is to become a whole person. To be able to love and respect your own reality, callipers, disabilities and all, you have to love and respect yourself first. For example, I love to laugh really loud and with joy and not take myself too seriously, but for a long long time, I allowed society to make me a lesser person than who I was supposed to be. Society did not understand my laugh. For them this was not the picture that fitted a crippled girl. I was always reminded not to laugh so loud. Today I realise that they envied my laughter and wanted to project their insecurities about themselves onto me.

I also believe that sensuality is a journey towards this acceptance of yourself. To feel comfortable in your own skin is very sensuous. My journey towards being sensual and in control of my body started with accepting my own laughter, my zest for life, my own sense of rhythm. And this journey started when I decided: I accept everything, I blame no one, and the world owes me nothing.

Qualifications:
I obtained a B. Mus and a B.Ed. degree from the University of the Western Cape. I also completed a Senior Management Diploma at the University of Stellenbosch.

Occupation:
I am the director of Audience Development and Education at Artscape.

Commissions & Organisations:
At the end of 2003, I was appointed by President Thabo Mbeki to be a Commissioner on one of the Chapter 9 commissions – The Commission for the protection of the Rights of Cultural, Religious and Linguistic Communities.

I have served the following organisations:
- Sigma Health: director
- CYT Certificate of Youth Trainers – a skills and leadership programme sponsored by the French Foreign Ministry: chairperson, 2002– present
- Black Management Forum: executive member, 2003 – April 2005
- Western Cape Cultural Commission: chairperson, 2001– 2005
- Golden Arrow Foundation: chairperson, 1998 – 2004
- Direct Marketing Organisation: member of the board, 2003 – 2004
- Development Education Trust Western Cape Education Department: member, 2001– 2002

- RDP forum in Kuilsrivier: chairperson, 1992 –1998
- SIDA (Swedish International Development Agency) responsible for exchange programmes and advisor to arts programmes in the previous disadvantaged communities of the Western Cape: coordinator, 1996
- British Council UK Disability Forum: representative, 2002.

Awards:
- Shoprite/Checkers Woman of the Year Award (Arts and Culture Category) – 1998
- Desmond Tutu Legendary Award – 2001
- Chevalier Des Ordres Et Des Lettres (French knighthood in the Performing Arts) – 2002
- Recipient of the Woman of the World Path the Way Award – 2004
- Western Cape Provincial Award (Arts and Culture)
- Honorary Member of the Golden Key Chapter, University of Stellenbosch – 2007
- Alumnus of the Year award, University of Stellenbosch Business School – 2007

Contact details:
email: marlenel@artscape.co.za
cell: 083 701 8889
tel: 021 410 9958

Painting of me by Manfred Zylla

83

Born a diva

With my mom, Tittie

Me with Tittie, Ma Christie and the aunts

Ma Christy with all the cousins

Marlene's album

With friends, Lexy and Caureen

In the church choir

With my partner

My gorgeous children, Adam and Aimee

I was a happy child because my parents treated me like any other child: I was expected to do household chores and other things that come with the responsibility of being a first-born child.

« Un manque d'oxygène fut à l'origine de mon handicap. […] Les gens du centre d'examen d'entrée à l'université ne pouvaient pas déchiffrer mon écriture. J'ai donc échoué deux fois. […] J'ai alors écrit en utilisant mes mains et ensuite demandé à quelqu'un de retranscrire ce que je venais d'écrire. Cette fois-ci, j'ai obtenu mon certificat.»

Achève son diplôme en Management Public et Développement. Débuta dans un concours de beauté pour Miss Confiance. Directrice de « Tinyungubyiseni Talent Promotions », de « I Can Events » et lauréate de nombreuses récompenses en 2004, 2005 et 2006.

Three years before my birth, my mother had a miscarriage and was told that there was a possibility she would never be able to have children again. As if this was not enough for her, I was born on 24 October 1978, and a lack of oxygen resulted in my disability. I was diagnosed with cerebral palsy. However, my parents were not aware of my disability until I was about two years old. At this stage they realised that I was not developing at the same pace as the other children of my age. I was taken from one doctor to another and eventually they were told about my disability.

I went to a school for children with cerebral palsy at Baragwanath Hospital (Johannesburg), but it was difficult for my parents because they were based in Giyani (Limpopo). After consultations it was agreed that I could attend an ordinary school in Giyani. I passed Grade 1, but failed Grade 2 because the teachers couldn't read my handwriting.

Luckily, one special teacher decided to go through my books because she could not understand how I could be so eloquent in speaking but not translate that into writing. She discovered that people just didn't make an effort to go through what I had written, because she could tell there was nothing wrong with my intellect. My poor parents had to go and explain the situation every time I went to a new class. I went to a normal school until Grade 7.

I was a happy child, because my parents treated me like any other child. I was expected to do household chores and other things that come with the responsibility of being a firstborn child. When I was with my playmates I was able to convince them to change the rules and the structure of the games we played to accommodate me. It was easier for me to be around children than adults, because the children didn't discriminate against me and they saw me as one of them. Although it never affected me, the adults always made remarks about how cruel my parents were, because they made me do household chores. In the end, my disability was harder on my parents than it was on me.

Although I was happy at school, I was not allowed to take part in some of the extramural activities like debate and drama. It was said that they couldn't understand my speech. This made my parents decide to take me to a special high school. I went to Filadelfia Secondary School from Grade 8. It was here that I actually realised how different I was from other people. For the first time since birth, I became sensitive about my disability.

When I got to Filadelfia, I was given a typewriter, because again they said they could not read my writing. I was not comfortable with this, so in Grade 9 I asked to stop using it. When I got to Grade 10 I chose science subjects because I understood them better. This was something that many students with cerebral palsy had been advised against because it was not practical to write science subjects using a typewriter. I wrote the final examination of matric using my hands, but the people at the marking centre couldn't read my handwriting and so I failed matric twice. We tried to find a solution to this problem with the Department of Education, but we were sent from pillar to post. We ended up consulting a lawyer and going to the premier's office and finally the matter was resolved. I wrote using my hands and then someone rewrote what I had written. This time I got my matric certificate.

Failing matric was very traumatic for me and my family, so the last thing

I wanted after that was to study further. I had to decide what I wanted to do with my life. The only thing I knew was I wanted to make a difference. The question now was how I was going to do it.

I had always wanted to be a beauty queen, so I decided to start a beauty pageant for people with disabilities. I called the pageant Miss Confidence South Africa. It was difficult in the beginning, because people didn't think that people with disabilities would partake, but I knew it could happen. I never got sponsorship for the first event but I was determined to make it happen and I did. Although there were many people who were skeptical about the pageant, there were always people who believed in me. Through their support and encouragement and through my faith in God I was able to carry on.

I started a company called Tinyungubyiseni Talent Promotions, since I needed a vehicle to run Miss Confidence South Africa. The company creates events to develop and empower people with disabilities. It was through the company's projects that people started to notice me and I gained some prominence.

When I won the Shoprite/Checkers Woman of the Year Award in 2004, doors started to open for me and the pageant. I got better sponsorship deals and the pageant got a lot of media attention. The battle for us has only been half-won because the ultimate achievement would be when people change their attitudes towards people with disabilities.

I went on to be voted one of the top ten women in South Africa for 2004, won the Amstel Salute to Success in 2005, was nominated Cosmopolitan Mover and Shaker of the Year 2005 and was one of the Cosmopolitan Awesome Women of the Year in 2006.

I am now doing a certificate in Public and Development Management, so that I can qualify for a master's degree. I am a shareholder and director in three other companies.

I still feel that people with disabilities are faced with twice the amount of obstacles. They are reminded daily that they are different from others, but despite this disadvantage they should be able to go out and conquer new challenges every day. I would like to see people with disabilities in leadership positions and owning their own businesses. I believe that we are not yet economically empowered. Even affirmative action has not made much of a difference in the lives of the disabled. Decisions are still made for us and I would like to see that change.

In the last five years, I have seen myself grow into a very powerful business woman, but one who will never forget where she came from. One who will strive to always help others, never forgetting that she herself is blessed.

Profile

Qualifications:
I completed matric.

Occupation:
I am the Managing Director of Tinyungubyiseni Talent Promotions and Director of I Can Events.

Achievements:
I won the Shoprite/Checkers Woman of the Year Award 2004 (Arts and Culture), was named one of the top ten women in South Africa for 2004 by the *Star*, won the Amstel Salute to Success 2005, was a Diva Award 2005 nominee for Cosmopolitan Mover of the Year 2005 and one of the Cosmopolitan Awesome Women for 2006.

Contact details:
email: missconfidencesa@gmail.com
tel: 011 941 1877
cell: 083 693 4718

In the last five years, I have seen myself grow into a very powerful business woman, but one who will never forget where she came from. One who will strive to always help others, never forgetting that she herself is blessed.

If you want to know how I have been saved, listen to my story. Jesus is my Saviour, He has given me life.

Matshidiso Elda Seboni

Paraplegic

My name is Matshidiso Elda Seboni. I had a very memorable childhood. I was a bubbly child and I am told that when I was a baby, I crawled on my bum. You can imagine how many nappies I ruined!

I took ill while I was in Grade 9 at a Catholic boarding school. It was a Saturday morning, but nobody took my condition seriously. The following Sunday I was woken up early to get ready for the eight o'clock church service. I was in a very bad state and I could not stand. Since I had no balance, I had to wash outside and I was shivering badly from a high fever. The next thing I remember is struggling to walk down a flight of stairs after church.

A friend phoned my parents in Pretoria and the following day my dad arrived at the school. He found me in hospital and I was delirious. He was deeply concerned about my condition. I could hardly recognise him and the things I said disturbed him so much that he wanted to take me to Pretoria General Hospital. The doctor who was attending to me refused and said he was busy conducting tests to determine the cause of my condition.

The following morning my dad was informed that I was suffering from typhoid fever and that I couldn't be transferred to Pretoria as St Rita's (the hospital where I was admitted) could handle the condition. My dad was prepared to hire a helicopter to fly me to Pretoria, but the hospital authorities refused.

St Rita's was a stone's throw away from my school and it was under-staffed and lacked resources. My condition deteriorated to such an extent that some so-called 'senior doctors' wanted to let nature take its course. Dr Sultan, who was attending to me, took a different stand and fought tooth and nail to save my life.

When my parents visited me in hospital they found a slight improve-ment in my condition. My dad was excited about the positive change, but my mom – who was seeing me for the first time – was upset and concerned. When my parents left the hospital I fell into a coma which lasted for 21 days. I had pneumonia in both lungs and my kidneys were not functioning well.

The doctors informed my parents that I was in a critical state and that they had to prepare themselves for the worst. My mom and grand-mother stayed with me for three weeks. My dad phoned daily to enquire about my condition. Thanks to God and Dr Sultan, I eventually came out of the coma. My mom and grandmother left for Pretoria and my dad came and stayed with me, until I was transferred to Tembisa Hospital for physiotherapy.

One interesting incident at St Rita's was when my sister and two brothers came to visit me. We took a family photo and when they left, I asked them to sing hymn 273 from the United Reformed Church in Southern Africa

(URCSA) hymnal. Neither I nor my parents remembered the words. I am told that they jumped with joy when they read the words in Sesotho which, translated into English are: 'If you want to know how I have been saved, listen to my story. Jesus is my Saviour, He has given me life.'

When I was admitted to Tembisa Hospital I could not sit up, use my hands or walk, and my speech was not clear. Through therapy I was able to regain seventy-five per cent of my physical strength and with continued therapy I am proud to say that I have now regained ninety per cent of my body strength. I am a paraplegic and I walk with crutches. I also have a tremor in both hands, but my speech has improved tremendously.

I did my Grade 10 at Holy Trinity High School in Atteridgeville. I was still weak at that time and my parents suggested that I spend the year attending to my therapy. I just could not deal with the idea of not being in school, so although it was tough, I went to school. I remember when my dad took me to a neurologist in an attempt to find medical advice about my condition. The neurologist told him not to waste his time with me because I was going to be a vegetable for the rest of my life. He said this in my presence and I burst out crying. At that point I decided that this was the beginning of a long journey ahead and I was ready to take it.

The following year I registered for Grades 11 and 12 simultaneously at Promat College. The teachers were excellent, except for the maths teacher who told me to my face that with my physical condition I could not take maths. But my test marks were always good. At first I was very upset, but decided to work harder and prove her wrong.

I passed matric and went on to register at Vista University for a B.Com. degree. It was difficult, since the campus was not accommodating for people with physical disabilities. I was made to write my exams in the admin block where the staff carried on with their everyday work and did not take my presence into consideration. It made it very hard for me to concentrate, and I decided to apply to the Oral Roberts University in Utah, USA. I received my application forms which I excitedly and confidently completed, but my parents refused to sign the forms. I felt that they were being overprotective and I needed to get out of my sheltered environment. They had their fears and were not ready to let me venture out on my own. So I registered with Unisa for a B.Com. degree. I tried to get into study groups, but I was rejected by my fellow students. I think it was because of my disability and their uninformed perceptions about disabled persons. Again the stereotype pushed me to work harder and my father became my study partner. He used to help me by taking notes during discussion classes and I used a tape recorder. I did my degree in four years using a typewriter for my exams. The tremor in my hands made it difficult and I typed with one finger. I have always believed that where there is a will, there is a way.

I furthered my studies at Access College, a vocational training centre for disabled people in Randburg. Before Access I was very shy, but there I met people with all kinds of disabilities and I was overwhelmed by how they were dealing with their conditions. About ninety-five per cent of the students had had their disabilities from infancy.

During the time I spent at Access I discovered that there was a world out there full of proudly disabled people. This was when I started to make peace with my disability. I became the assistant secretary of the Student Representative Council and I was actively involved in a feeding scheme where we prepared sandwiches for needy students.

Currently I am studying towards an honour's degree in Development Studies at Unisa.

Getting a driver's licence was a nightmare. I failed my first driver's licence because it was said that I took longer than required to do my yard test. I took my second test at a different centre, but it was no better. The officer questioned my ability to drive before even testing me. He said he was not keen to test me if I was a risk to other road users. I failed again. So I went to a third centre. Again the officer was sceptical, but I was determined to leave the centre with that precious document in my hands. I did everything according to the book, but she had problems with me driving barefeet. She insisted that it was illegal. To prevent an argument, I referred her to a gentleman who gave me permission at the traffic head office. I was then tested and I passed. Today I proudly and confidently drive myself, in my own vehicle.

My first day at my first job was nerve-wrecking. I was worried about whether I would cope and how my new colleagues would receive me. To my surprise I was given a warm welcome and my disability was not an issue at all. I did my work as expected and made friends. I stayed with my first employer for two years and three months.

In 1995 I started at my second job and there I also coped very well. In 2002 the company came under new management and things changed for the better. I do my work diligently and timeously and I am actively involved in the social club, HIV/Aids and occupational health and safety committees. I raised my concerns about the building not being accessible and today a brand new ramp at the entrance to the building is nearing completion. The toilet facilities and the auditorium are also being made wheelchair friendly. What I have noticed through my life as a disabled person is that one must take the lead in showing people how one expects to be treated. I do not pity myself and therefore I do not expect pity from other people, only respect. My colleagues and managers treat me like everybody else and that makes me very happy.

Relationships I found to be intriguing and confusing. I have met many men who showed interest in me, but the minute we started talking seriously, I discovered that they had approached me out of pity and nothing else. There were times when men would show interest in me while I was driving or seated (be it in my car or at a restaurant). The minute they saw how I walked, their interest would vanish. Others thought they were doing me a favour by approaching me.

My mom used to tell me not to worry, for I always looked beautiful and one day someone would come into my life and help celebrate that

beauty. I have now met Mr H who meets all my expectations in a partner and our relationship is based on respect, love and understanding. He is very supportive in everything I do and I appreciate having him in my life.

My other relationships are those with my close friends and colleagues (Morongwa, Kedibone, Mojabeng, Motlalepula, Bakae, Nina, Tebogo, Eva, and Lesley). These women have helped me to unearth my inner strength in ways that no words can describe. They attribute their acceptance of my disability to the way I view myself: not feeling sorry for myself.

I have a very strong relationship with my family. They have sacrificed a lot just to see me happy. As for my nieces and nephews, they have helped me to face some of the challenges. A good example is when we would go shopping and, as always, people would stare at me in a patronising way. My niece would then tell them loudly that it is rude to stare.

My journey through life as a disabled person was made easy by the strong family support I have. They have been my pillar of strength. My friends are always encouraging me to do whatever I want to do. I have a sister, friend and role model in Sebe. She has been an inspiration to me.

I have discovered that all the hassles and challenges I met on this journey of self-discovery have made me a stronger person. My confidence has improved tenfold and I am more assertive. I have also come to terms with the fact that the stereotypes will always be there and that it is up to me to always hold my head high and walk tall.

I have discovered that all the hassles and challenges I met on this journey of self-discovery have made me a stronger person. My confidence has improved tenfold and I am more assertive. I have also come to terms with the fact that the stereotypes will always be there and that it is up to me to always hold my head high and walk tall.

Profile

Qualifications:
I obtained a qualification from Guardian Angels' College and did a computer course for disabled at Access College.

Occupation:
I am the director at Divuseni Holdings (Pty) Ltd, a business initiative run by disabled women.

Hobbies:
Reading magazines and newspapers, driving, cooking, and doing things for myself.

Contact details:
email: sebonim@saasta.ac.za
tel: 012 392 9329
cell: 082 786 1881

Matshidiso's album

Photos of me throughout my life ...

It took some persuading to convince me to contribute to this book. Purely because I saw myself as an inappropriate subject. I am on the wrong side of fifty and definitely on the wrong side of eighty kilograms.

I find it incredibly sad that I have to feel like this. Like I am almost not worthy of being in a publication such as this. I put the blame for this a hundred per cent on the shoulders of the media. They portray a certain image of what a woman should be like and they dictate what women should look like. They define what sensuality is and millions of people buy into this, without ever questioning it.

The media brainwashes society into believing that in order to be valued, to matter, it is necessary to be young, slim, beautiful and most importantly, to be whole. If you have any defect, even a small one like a mole in the wrong place, you are not desirable. My problem is not a misplaced mole; I am blind. And when last did you see a spread in a magazine showcasing beautiful blind women, or any disabled woman for that matter? Disability is never made out to be beautiful.

As part of my current job, I often find myself advising young people with disabilities, and interestingly enough, most often young women. I tell them that the most important part of growing up is learning to embrace your disability as the most essential part of who you are. This is much easier said than done, especially when you are eighteen and yearning to fit in, to belong and to be desired. The irony lies in the fact that the devices you have to use to make your way in the world – your white cane, your crutches, your wheelchair – are the very things that high-light your difference and heighten your status as undesirable. We all find ways of minimising this sense of unworthiness, because I don't think there is a single disabled person who doesn't suffer from this feeling their whole life.

Looking back on my life, I wish I had chosen a more profitable, more useful way of proving to the world that I did matter, that I did have value, that I was worth loving. Instead, I chose an arena in which the limitations of disability would be neutralised. I realised that there was at least one thing that I could do as well as, if not better than, the girls who could see. Being a great lover did not require eyesight. I had enough other senses that worked perfectly fine and I began to see this as an incredible strength. Sometimes I wonder if there is a much darker side to this belief. That I was somehow subtly persuaded that this was all I was good for, rather than good at?

A man whom I will always remember with the most profound tenderness once paid me the following compliment. He said: 'I read somewhere that in the eighteenth century they used to make canaries blind so that that they would sing more beautifully. I believe God made you blind in order to make you a better lover.'

I have to admit that whether it was God's intention or not, for much of my life I worked hard at being a good lover. Although one would assume that if God indeed had a plan for the people he disabled, it would be for a less frivolous purpose. God really works in mysterious ways.

Yet loving is what I'm good at for now. No longer in the physical sense, though; loving the whole world out there now has become my forte. Loving the people I interact with on a daily basis: my colleagues at university, the students we serve, my family and my friends. And then also people I encounter randomly, like strangers as they assist me across the street. It doesn't occur to me to wonder if they love me back. Mercifully, as we get older, the craving for being loved diminishes and one is freer to love without requiring that love be reciprocated.

Maybe the canary metaphor is not such a bad one and maybe it is what God had intended. That I should learn to love without requiring that it be returned.

A man whom I will always remember with the most profound tenderness once paid me the following compliment. He said: `I read somewhere that during the eighteenth century they used to make canaries blind so that they would sing more beautifully. I believe God made you blind in order to make you a better lover.`

Profile

Occupation:
I work at the UCT Disability Unit.

Contact details:
email: popplestone@telkomsa.net
tel: 021 650 5090
cell: 083 456 4700

Little Reinette

In my wilder days

Ready for the date

love children

My little girl

I dared to open doors
I learnt to fight my fears
Looking at my situation
There was so much I could do
And it all depended on me to
find my way back
to get on the track
to learn to fly
and to soar above all doubts

« Un lourd bang. [...] Puis le silence. Le son d'une sirène. Le silence. [...] Je réalisais que nous venions d'avoir un accident. [...] Ma 7ème vertèbre cervicale avait été touchée. [...] A cause de cet accident, Matthew [son fils, ndlr] a subi des lésions cérébrales. Il ne peut plus parler. Il vit dans son propre monde. »

Mariée, deux enfants.
Aime la poésie.
Division de la conformité des programmes à eTV.

ROSS
Hullins
T e t r a p l e g i c

Beginning something new
Like writing on a blank space
A mystery unfolding
Right in front of your face
It is a story
That has never been told
I would like you to know
How it feels to begin something new
To leave things behind
And let it all unfold
For the world to see
And now you can know

Sunday morning. The day started like any other ordinary Sunday. We were invited for a braai at our friend's house. I offered to make my special rice salad and a healthy, crispy fresh green salad. I was six months pregnant. I was rushing, because my firstborn Stephanie had started primary school, and her school uniform had to be ironed before we could leave. In my haste, I suddenly dropped the bowl with the rice salad and it fell in countless pieces as if it was a foreboding omen. I picked up the pieces, swept up the mess, washed the floor and off we went to lunch.

This was one of those days we refer to as a 'stinker', meaning it was very hot. We had a great lunch, while the kids nagged to go to the beach for ice cream. Finally we agreed to take them in my friend's brand new car. The men were seated in front and my friend Michelle, the three children and I were seated in the back.

A loud bang. I heard Michelle screaming 'Evan!' Then silence. The sound of a siren. Silence. A very inquisitive crowd, whispering. Silence. Sounds of more sirens. Silence. I was drunk with confusion.

I realised we had been in an accident. By then there were paramedics on the scene. I heard the two paramedics chatting: the one said to the other: 'Cut the belt'. The other one said: 'He's not going to make it, he lost too much blood'. I tried to make sense of all this – they were talking about my husband. He was bleeding so much that his blood dripped on a bundle of clothes underneath his seat. I realised that the bundle of clothes was actually my baby, Stephanie. She was so tiny and fragile. I was scared. I was scared for her, for my husband Sidney, for my unborn child, and I was scared for myself. I could see my family slipping away and I could not help any of them. I don't think I have ever prayed so hard. I was not ready to say goodbye to them and God complied: they all survived. But my world came to a stop.

I was lifted into an ambulance and rushed off to hospital. The X-rays confirmed that I had severed my seventh cervical vertebra. I was to be operated on the next day, but my fever was too high and it was postponed. I celebrated my 30th birthday in ICU. I felt so empty, so alone and so scared.

When the doctors finally operated, they were not completely successful. I had to stay in bed on my back for six weeks. My hospital bed became my home. I was there to live or to die and my existence made no sense. Just as I was stabilised and ready to be transferred to another ward, I suddenly fell ill. Doctors and nurses were very worried. I knew something was wrong and I thought I was dying. I was rushed off to Tygerberg

Hospital. My water broke and I went into premature labour. This was not good – I was not due for another two months. At 9 am I gave birth to a tiny little man, so frail and fragile. The doctors were amazed, as they did not think I would be able to give birth naturally.

After four months of rehab I was allowed to go home for a weekend. I was both scared and excited, fearful and anxious. The night before I went home I could not sleep.

Surrounded by noise
Trapped without sound
I'm lost in confusion
As I look around
I write this all down
With nothing to do
Scared and alone
I need you!
I need who?
I need what?
I need me!

It was a cold weekend, and everyone tried to make me feel at home, but their fussing made me feel even more cold and uncomfortable. Nothing could warm me, not even the baby shower they had arranged with all my friends. I was grateful for the thought, but upset because I was not ready to face people and I had to smile and pretend to be happy. I could not wait for it all to end.

I did not want to be a burden on my friends and family. I secretly decided to book myself into a home where other people would take care of me.

Sunday evening when I went back to hospital it felt like going home. The sheltered environment made me feel safe. I asked the staff to help me find a home for people with disabilities. All the homes we called were full and had long waiting lists. Even if I did get a place I would not be able to afford it. I had no income. I was broke. I had nothing. I was a

nothing. After eight months of rehab I was discharged.

During my first days at home all I did was sit in the sun, rest, sleep and eat. I was tired of being me, tired of being dependent on others and I felt like I had nothing to live for. I did not even want to take care of my kids. I felt I had lost my dignity, my independence and my pride.

As the days went by I promised myself that I would claim all this back. I had no clue how I was going to do it. I had two young children who depended on me. I wanted to see them grow up. They needed me and this made me realise that my pain was not mine alone. Others shared in it as well. I had to start believing in myself again.

The most difficult part of being disabled is coming to terms with the negative thoughts you internalise.

My journey today, my journey tomorrow
I may feel sorrow
But I'll wait till tomorrow for another
chance to continue my journey
I want to live for another tomorrow.
I have problems, lots of problems
I have stops and detours
but it's how I pull through
that makes my journey.
It's the troubles I face
that can make my journey great,
so I'll
travel until the end
because my journey may
find something great!

I made a mental decision that the things that made life worth living were love, family, friends and laughter. Love makes us feel wanted and needed. With family we share precious moments. Friends are there to hold you up when you fall down. Laughter is considered to be the best medicine. I also think one more important thing in life is to know who you are. To feel comfortable with yourself and to be proud of what you have achieved in life.

I had to say to myself: Ross Mullins, you are a great woman! You have substance, integrity, dignity and pride. You have a family, you have friends, you know how to laugh and most of all you know yourself very well . . .

> Beneath my skin a hopeful spirit echoed
> Asking me to be faithful to myself
> To reach out and touch my pain
> To humbly love
> To torture my fears
> To let go of my burdens
> And to take control

Before long Sidney and I moved out of my mother's place and into our own house. I joined the organisation Disabled People South Africa (DPSA) to interact with other disabled people. I started working at a government project for nature conservation. I served on their employment equity board and initiated and developed a tailor-made employment equity document for them. This was to ensure that we employed more people with different disabilities to reasonably accommodate them. I joined the South African Qualifications Authority (SAQA) and I served on their national standard board for law and military science and security. To attend their meetings I travelled to Pretoria for three days every two months. I also assisted a project manager with the organising of a visibility arts festival. Once I had started, it seemed as if there was no stopping me. And I loved it.

One of the things that I wanted to do was to be independent and mobile. I was constantly depending on people to take me places. Waiting on lifts became very frustrating. Because I am a tetraplegic, I was scared to attempt driving. I could not handle more disappointment. I scraped up all my courage and asked a friend if I could borrow her car to have

a few lessons. What a glorious delight. I got behind the wheel and it was as if I had never stopped driving. I got myself a brand new car and started a new job as a compliance advisor for a TV channel. We bought a new house and tried to make it as accessible as possible.

> I dared to open doors
> I learnt to fight my fears
> Looking at my situation
> There was so much I could do
> And it all depended on me to
> find my way back
> to get on the track
> to learn to fly
> and to soar above all doubts

My children grew up so fast. Stephanie started high school and it was time for us to find Matthew a school. Matthew is our special child. Because of my accident Matthew sustained brain damage. He is not verbal at all. He lives in a world of his own. These two children make life worth living. I love spending time with them. They make me realise that I am needed. They give me a sense of worthiness. They love unconditionally. They have taught me how to be confident.

I know that Sidney was also thrown in the deep end when he had to face my and Matthew's disability. I sometimes forget to thank him for all he has done. We have a bond of mutual loss.

Then there is my mother. What an amazing woman. Out of nowhere, with no warning, she had a thirty-year-old baby. She handled it like a pro. She could only see the positive in me. She cured my broken spirit with her gentle words.

We live our life in phases. Change is constant and life is short, so we must seize the moment and live life to the fullest. I have accepted what has happened to me and this has enabled me to embark on a whole new start.

Maintaining a healthy sex life after my spinal cord injury was an important priority to me. People with disabilities are often regarded as non-sexual adults. Sex is very much associated with youth and physical attraction. If sex and disability are discussed, it is in terms of capacity, technique, and fertility – in particular, male capacity and technique, and female fertility – with no reference to sexual feelings or sensuality.

I would like to challenge the myths that disabled people are invisible, asexual, undesirable or incapable. I would like to break down stereotypes, raising awareness and mainly inspiring those with disabilities to understand and appreciate their sexuality.

Of course I still want to experience pleasure! Pleasure is an affirmation of life. The significance of sexual pleasure refers to pleasure as 'the authentic, abiding satisfaction that makes us feel like complete human beings'. And I see myself as complete. Sexual pleasure enhances my intimate relationship with my partner. It can help build my immunity against media messages that make me feel as if I don't deserve pleasure. Life has handed me a raw deal, but when I sit back and count my blessings I do not feel pain. I am alive and living a full life. I would not change this life for another. I am at peace. I will remember and cherish every day of my life. I will love every day that I have the opportunity to breathe and to live.

You place your hands on my broken spine
And you feel my spirit in whole.
Slowly our tongues wrestle in our mouths ...
And you know my soul is alive.
The passion I feel makes me feel like a woman ...
The way you look at me when we are done, makes me feel
like a woman ...
Nothing is incomplete about me
The way you caress every curve of my body, makes me feel
like a woman ...

Every curve, every line on me comes alive
I feel like a woman, I am a woman
The way you tickle my neck with your tongue ever so
gently, makes me feel like a woman ...
Our bodies touching, melting and moulding into perfection,
makes me feel like a woman ...
The love that we share, the time that we share, and the
things that we share makes me feel like a woman.
I am woman; I feel like a woman, I am alive!

Profile

Occupation:
I work at e.tv, in the programme compliance division.

Hobbies:
I enjoy writing poetry.

Contact details:
email: ross.mullins@etv.co.za
tel: 021 481 4560
cell: 083 867 6167

Ross's album

My wedding day

My son

After the accident

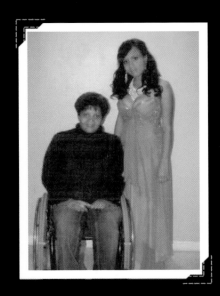

My daughter

« Je me rappelle la première fois où ma sœur m'a amenée dans un centre de santé pour que j'ai accès aux moyens contraceptifs. L'infirmière lui a reproché d'amener à la clinique une fille handicapée. […] Dans leur esprit, j'étais paraplégique et donc asexuée. […] Mon premier enfant fut une magnifique fille, petite Hleziphi, qui malheureusement mourut après seulement 5 jours sur cette terre. […] La douleur n'est jamais réellement partie. »

Mère célibataire de deux fils.
Biométricienne qualifiée.
Etudia et voyagea principalement pour la promotion des partenariats en faveur des personnes invalides, à la fois localement et internationalement. Directrice exécutive du « African Access Holdings » et intérêts particuliers dans l'entreprise « Diveseni » qui œuvre pour le renforcement du pouvoir des femmes invalides.

Sebenzile Matsebula

Paraplegic

I came into a family that already had six children. So my wonderful mother decided that she had done her job for the Matsebula family and she called me 'Sebenzile' meaning 'I have worked'. That name was also a forecast for my life, which has been filled by the hectic schedule of a professional. But then this busy life has also been enriched by very interesting, exciting, sad, horrific, elating and fulfilling episodes.

I was born on 23 September 1957 in the dusty town of Barberton. During my school years the only social exposure I had was with my family. I led a very sheltered life. Life was about going to school, spending time at home and visiting family in various parts of Swaziland and South Africa. In fact, there was very little entertainment besides these family events and parties. In those days, life as a young woman with a disability was not very exciting, so you can imagine that my first encounter of love was an unforgettable and beautiful experience of sheer innocence. It was with a young man from Soweto who was a student in Swaziland.

I was very lucky to be the youngest of five sisters, and so support for my transition from childhood into womanhood came from every angle, including my very caring and loving mother. But despite all this loving care, I had to learn that the world outside my sheltered family was where I would have to face the public prejudice. I remember the first day my sister took me to a health clinic for birth control: the nurses chided her for bringing a disabled girl to the clinic for birth control. What was she thinking? The nurses knew my sister very well, but they simply could not understand why I needed birth control. In their minds I was disabled and therefore asexual. My sister is a very bright woman and she saw beyond the narrow minds of the nurses and believed that as a young woman, I deserved and needed protection. But this was back in the seventies and

I never got any birth control from those wretched nurses.

The saddest thing is that even today you will hear young girls with disabilities recount similar stories. People's attitudes and perceptions toward women with disabilities have changed very little. When will people realise that women with disabilities are women first and then disabled?

When I left home to attend university in 1979 a whole new world opened. I was in residence and shared a room. Even though the students were very good to me, I never really felt a part of the social structure, as I was the only person on campus with a disability. So I dedicated my life to study. During my first degree I had occasional relationships, which were not fulfilling, as I was always asked to keep things secret. It was not cool to be seen in public with a disabled woman. When there was the occasional campus ball, the world was not a comfortable place for me to be in.

It was only when I went to the United States to do my master's degree that I experienced a side of life that I have never been part of before: parties, clubbing and fun. It was there that I had my first real love experience. It was a very intense relationship, but alas, it ended in a very abusive situation. Over the years, this was becoming a pattern. I went through a couple of relationships, and in the end I sadly realised that none of them had been genuine. At some point they would always turn physical and then it would be about providing for someone else's needs more than mine. Later, as I progressed in life and had a good job with a big salary, the relationships were usually linked to my financial success, all going nowhere. Today I am alone, but I will forever rejoice that the children born as rewards from my past relationships, were born out of love.

My first child was a beautiful girl, little Hleziphi, who sadly passed away after only five days on earth. It is the most horrific thing that any human being can experience. Even though it happened decades ago in 1984, the pain has never completely gone. But over the years, the intensity has lessened and one learns to get on with life. The God that I worship certainly has a wonderful remedy to heal broken hearts and the girl was followed by two beautiful boys, Mpendulo and Thando. Each of my pregnancies was a beautiful experience, even though my second one was rather hectic. I developed pre-eclampsia and ended up in bed for a total of four months, doing nothing except visiting the doctor and the loo. The last one was easy. Carrying a heavy bump and extra weight on my crutches was rather tricky, but I marvelled at God's ingenuity of getting me through it all in one piece.

Learning to take care and carry a baby whilst struggling with crutches was another challenge, but I made the best of it. There were occasions when I had to carry my baby on my back (as is common with African women). Now, when you have a heavy frame like I do, carrying a heavy baby on your back and trying to balance on crutches is quite a feat. But I just had to do it and where there is a will, there is always a way. My two boys are now 22 and 18 and are the greatest pleasure that I have ever had. They give true meaning to my life. Over the years they have been my motivation that keep me grounded and continuously remind me that life is about sharing and giving. What beautiful gifts they are!

Maturity brought new insights. I became part of a wider circle of people with disabilities, and I found myself able to enjoy partying and dancing until the early hours of the morning. Being a person with a disability is no longer an issue when I am on the dance floor (even when I am the only disabled person on the dance floor). Maturity is a beautiful part of life as it liberates you. It enables you to enjoy the now as if there is no tomorrow, and it has made me realise that the myth about the sexuality of women with disabilities can only be dispelled by women with disabilities themselves. Women with disabilities are indeed highly sexual and enjoy intimacy just as much as any other person does.

I believe that I am a beautiful creation of God. I may not be physically attractive (whatever that means), but I believe my spirit and soul carries

a beauty that cannot be measured. It is this beauty that I wish to share with the rest of the world at every waking moment so that we can appreciate that we are very privileged human beings. Our disability is but a big bonus that we have, as we continue on the journey of life and continuous self-discovery.

Profile

Qualifications:
I received academic training in Biometrics and worked for 15 years as a Biometrician at a research institute. I have studied in Botswana, Canada, Swaziland and the United States of America and travelled extensively to promote disability rights and to forge links and partnerships with the international disability movement.

Occupation:
I am the executive director at African Access Holdings, a company which has committed to the economic empowerment of people with disabilities through a range of initiatives. More recently I mobilised disabled women who have business interests to form a company of disabled women that share a particular passion in business development as a vehicle to empower disabled women. The company is called Divuseni, meaning 'lift yourself up'.

Hobbies:
My passion for life is driven by learning. Hence I read every moment that I have. I believe that knowledge can make or break one in all aspects of one's development.

Contact details:
email: Sebe@divuseni.co.za
tel: 012 803 1409
cell: 082 905 0432

Sebenzile's album

A younger me

Me and my crutches

Graduation day

With my lovely kids

I am a firm believer in positive thinking and I have witnessed its full power in my life. I want to re-imagine my imagination, create a different way of seeing, writing, being. I am not interested in being like everybody else. I find that rather dull, actually.

I have come to realise that unless we (as people with disabilities) are able to be the maker of own images, our lives will constantly be depicted on the basis of the assumptions others hold of who we are, how we live, how we love.

Paraplegic

« À 24 ans, je me suis réveillée dans un hôpital, les murs étaient vides et mes rêves brisés. J'étais une victime de plus dans la célèbre guerre des taxis en Afrique du Sud. [...] Le tube enfoncé dans ma gorge, via une ouverture pratiquée dans ma trachée, me permettait de respirer et de parler. J'orne cette petite ouverture depuis plusieurs années maintenant, en portant des colliers fabriqués par ma mère. »

Master en Beaux Arts (Temple University, Philadelphia).
Lauréate de nombreuses récompenses pour des documentaires réalisés aux USA.
Enseignante en Cinéma à l'université de Witwatersrand depuis Juillet 2008, en fauteuil roulant.

I know about this dance of living. This dance is not with the feet. This dance is with the heart. And when I dance with the heart, music comes through me. Music is me. And then all that I am, is the dance.

At the age of 24, I woke up to find myself in hospital with empty walls and broken dreams. I was just another victim of the notorious taxi wars in South Africa.

Long before the doctors had the courage to admit it, my body had already told me: I was paralysed from the chest down. The utter colourlessness of those days made me contemplate the full extent of my loss: Never to be desired again. My body had become damaged goods; my sexuality erased. I was now part of those whom society prefers to ignore, and whom the media likes to portray as beggars or hospital patients. The mental picture I had of a person with disability was of someone in need of care, someone to be pitied, someone who certainly had no real claim to love or any kind of fulfilling life.

The first time I ventured out into the public domain, I was acutely aware of how different public engagement was. People now looked at me with pity or averted their gaze as I headed in their direction. Even some of my friends were not quite sure how to deal with the 'new' me. Some stayed away. Others came closer. I was still the old Shelley that everyone knew; Shelley with boundless energy, but I sensed a deep maturity within. Shelley was growing spiritually at a rapid rate.

My political consciousness grew within the disability rights movement. I began to acknowledge that it was society that had placed my body in a box with a label and stuck it away on a dusty shelf. I had a different body, yes. Not a damaged one.

The process of reclaiming my body was an exceptionally powerful and liberating experience. I understood desire and sensuality from a completely different perspective. I felt pride. I even dared to feel beautiful. I cruised around on my wheels feeling that I had every right to be in this world, as much as anyone else did. And I began to live with a passion and fervour that changed the course of my life in a fundamental way. But it has been a long route from there to here.

I initially qualified as an English and Drama teacher and taught in Cape Town and later in Japan. After being paralysed I became actively involved in the disability rights movement, working with the organisation Disabled People South Africa as their parliamentary officer. This was an incredible and daunting experience, but what a joy it was to be in Parliament post-1994, and to witness the growing changes, to instill some sense of disability awareness upon policy-makers and to meet all the comrades. The highlight of this time was organising Mandela's guard of honour for his state of the nation address. The guard was made up of people of various disabilities and all of us were invited to meet Madiba. This was the first time in South African history that a presidential speech had been delivered in sign language. It was an honour that will stay with me for eternity.

After the years in the disability rights movement, I was ready to return to my childhood dream of becoming a filmmaker . . .

I was raised in Korsten, Port Elizabeth. It was in no way an enchanting childhood, but certainly one that was never lacking in love. I had a mother who read me poetry, I practically lived in the local library and cinema, my father spoilt me rotten, my grandmothers loved me endlessly and my extended family was always there. I grew up during the years of apartheid in South Africa, so my dream of becoming a writer or filmmaker was an impossible one, yet never once did anyone in my family seem to think it was an absurd idea! I treasure this, deeply.

When people believe in you, there is very little that can stop you. This is the greatest treasure my parents have given me.

I was fortunate enough to receive a scholarship from the Ford Foundation and at the age of 32 I became a full-time student again. During my very first writing class at the Temple University in Philadelphia, my professor told us: 'Write about something because you just have to write about it. Write from your soul.'

My first film birthed itself with this honesty. I entitled it *Whole – A Trinity of Being*. It was a visual doc-poem of three short films, which explored my spiritual journey of embracing and celebrating my body. At last I had the opportunity to tell how the fabric of my life had been torn apart and what revelations had taken me beyond this loss. The film ends with a declaration of discovery. It has been years since making that first film. To date, it has won several international film awards, much to my surprise.

I choose not to wear the garment of bitterness so easily fitted to the wounded body. To date one of my biggest realisations has been the painful beauty that lies within touch, by knowing touch and not by feeling touch. I am not interested in only being touched on the non-paralysed parts of my body. My body is whole, not segmented into feeling and not-feeling. I recognise the pleasure of being touched and experiencing that touch on a mental and spiritual level, not a physical one. Interestingly enough, my most memorable and beautiful physical encounters were after the shooting – probably because of who I had grown into as a woman and how that had informed who I chose to be with. I had never been the kind of person to engage in physical pleasure for the sake of it. I always needed to be engaged spiritually and emotionally by someone. This had not changed, only intensified.

Another part of me that I had to come to terms with was the tube that fits into a hole in my throat allowing me to breathe and speak. I have been adorning this hole for several years now, wearing jewellery made by my mother, Pam, along with other artists. I celebrate this hole. The breath and speech it gives is my life force. So, I decorate it with jewellery, different handmade beads and trinkets, because scars should also be crowned. Even if they're not neat or pretty or are hard to look at sometimes.

My life in a wheelchair still claims a strong sense of sexuality, life force and desire. One of the hardest scenes I did for my film was a shot of my wheelchair next to where I am in the bath, cutting to a shot of my hands travelling over my body, in a gesture of masturbation. Doing this scene was not at all gratuitous. It was a political decision of painting a picture of a disabled woman who has an active sexual relationship with herself. In another scene, I depict my partner and I in a loving embrace. Difficult to do, simply because it pierces into my private world: yet the necessity far outweighed the difficulty. I have been in a long-term relationship with the sweetest woman on the planet and I feel exceptionally blessed. As time goes by I am amazed at how love deepens and is enriched by time and experience and how wonderful it is to discover someone in their entirety.

My work has continued to focus on re-envisaging a media that makes people with disabilities visible, not only as sexual beings but

as people in the fullness of human experience. I eventually realised my dreams of becoming a filmmaker and sometimes when I think about it, I am amazed by the possibilities we are all capable of, once we put aside negativity.

I am a firm believer in positive thinking and I have witnessed its full power in my life. I want to re-imagine my imagination, create a different way of seeing, writing, being. I am not interested in being like every-body else. I find that rather dull, actually.

I am currently exploring the cinematic aesthetics of filming from a seated position. It is a fact that when seated, the view of the world is quite different. I am eager for this to be another form of cinematography that will hopefully be seen as an art in itself. I will be working with the engineering department at Wits University to design equipment that will attach to my wheelchair, enabling me to film from that position. However, since I am not 'confined' to my wheelchair, I will also film from other seated positions: on cranes and from helicopters, for example. Instead of regarding my disability as a limitation in being a filmmaker, I have come to consider it as creating opportunities for a unique form of filmmaking. So much depends on your perspective.

I have started my own film company, Twospinningwheels Productions, and even though it is really tough right now, I know that with hard work and faith, I will one day have a successful business.

I am acutely aware that I am living in the midst of dreams unfolding.

I have come to realise that unless we (as people with disabilities) are able to be the maker of own images, our lives will constantly be depicted on the basis of the assumptions others hold of who we are, how we live, how we love.

Sections of this article initially appeared in Feminist Africa

Profile

Qualifications:
In 2003 I was awarded a full scholarship from the Ford Foundation to study towards my Master of Fine Arts in Film in the United States. I graduated cum laude from Temple University in Philadelphia.

Occupation:
The University of Witwatersrand in Johannesburg has recently announced that I have been selected as their Carnegie Fellow of 2007 in the TV and Film department. I will be based there from July, working on new films and on the aesthetics of cinematography from the perspective of a wheelchair user.

Awards:
I received the Audre Lorde Award for media, a Distinguished Graduate Student Award from the Pennsylvania Association of Graduate schools and three Best Film Awards at international festivals in NYC, San Francisco and Philadelphia for my first film, an experimental documentary entitled *Whole - A Trinity of Being*. This film has also been awarded the Jury Citation Award at the Black Maria Film Festival in the USA. The work-in-progress version of my thesis film *Where we planted trees* was recently awarded Best Documentary at Temple University's annual showcase of student films.

Contact details:
email: twospinningwheels@yahoo.com
tel: 041 3673618
cell: 072 329 4418
http//:www.shelleybarry.com

Being christened

Me as a kid

With my aunts

The whole family ...

Another part of me that I had to come to terms with was the tube that fits into a hole in my throat allowing me to breathe and speak. I have been adorning this hole for several years now, wearing jewellery made by my mother, Pam, along with other artists. I celebrate this hole.

Despite this incident/accident I came to terms with my disability, through family support and rehabilitation. The accident brought a whole new meaning to my marriage vows.

Soraya Scott

Wheelchair bound

« J'attendais que mon nom soit annoncé pour la remise du Prix 'The premier Of Gauteng's Woman of the Year for Economic Empowerment'. Un pan entier de la scène s'est effondré… Il y a eu des cris et de la confusion. Je me suis cassée le dos et suis devenue paralysée à partir du bas de la taille. »

Mariée, un enfant.
Maîtrise de Droit (Université de Cape Town).
Master de Droit (Université d'Afrique du Sud)
Certificat dans le secteur des assurances.
Lauréate du Prix « Premier's Womens of the Year Award for Economic Empowerment » en 2003.
Associée de l'équipe de conseil en droit et Finances Uranus.

On 9 August 2003, as part of the Women's Day celebrations, I was anxiously and proudly sharing a stage at the Union Buildings in Pretoria with the State President, the Premier of Gauteng and several other ministers and dignitaries. I was waiting for my name to be announced as the winner of The Premier of Gauteng's Women of the Year Award for Economic Empowerment. Then part of the stage collapsed …

There was shock and confusion. I broke my back and I was left paralysed from the waist down.

I was born in the Western Cape. My father came from Johannesburg, met my mother in Cape Town and got married at a very young age. I am the eldest of four sisters and will be turning 42 on 16 November 2007. I also had an elder brother who died of muscular dystrophy at the age of 16. Even though my brother died so young, the impact he made on my life was everlasting. He was extremely intelligent and displayed an amazing amount of wisdom for his age.

When I was 11 my family relocated to Johannesburg, where I finished matric at Chris J. Botha in 1984. I enrolled as a law student at the University of the Western Cape and completed a B.Juris. degree. During this time I became actively involved in the struggle against apartheid. My studies were constantly interrupted by my

commitment to this cause, which I am proud to say was worth every march, meeting and riot. My time at UWC will always remain one of the most meaningful experiences in my life.

I left Cape Town for Johannesburg in 1989. I was drowning in student debt, but was very excited to find a career in the City of Gold. During the nineties I held several jobs to support myself and settle my student loan. It was during this time that I married the love of my life, Isaac Scott, a fellow law student. Today we are the proud parents of an 11-year-old son.

I ventured into the business world as an entrepreneur in 2001 and established Xiphame Services. Its main objective was the economic empowerment of women in the waste management environment. The goal of the company was to bring waste management as a component of essential services to the millions of South Africans who were previously excluded from an adequate waste management system.

Xiphame Services penetrated the waste management field in August 2002, when it was awarded its first five-year contract with Pikitup Waste Management Utility in Gauteng, for the removal of illegal dumping in the south of Johannesburg. My career was on track and I was ready to conquer my next big business venture. That was when my life changed drastically …

During the last two years I have restructured my business to include other markets. Autumn Star Trading was established in 2005, which is a broad-based company consisting of women and disabled people. The company is primarily an investment company, with shareholdings in the IT, finance, mining and transport sectors.

Femweb Enterprises, an economic empowerment initiative, was established in 2005 and provides catering services, wedding planning, corporate functions and so on.

Uranus Consultancy was established in 2004 and consists of a group of professionals who provide legal services, auditing and financial accounting services.

Even though my career is still important, my first priority is my family, whom I love and value dearly. The accident also brought a whole new meaning to my marriage vows. A traumatic experience like this will either break or make a relationship. My marriage was tested on each and every level possible, but with the help of my family, and quite a lot of rehabilitation, I can honestly say that I have come to terms with my disability.

Profile

Qualifications:
I have a B.Juris. degree (University of the Western Cape), a Diploma in Law (Unisa) and a Certificate in Insurance Sector: Annuities, Policy Valuations, Mediation and Arbitrations and Conflict Handling.

Occupation:
I am an associate of Uranus Consulting, a legal and financial team handling investigations at municipalities and provincial government.

Awards:
In August 2003 I was the recipient of the Premier's Women of the Year Award for Gauteng in respect of economic empowerment.

Soraya's album

As a little girl ...

With my cute son

I still struggle to come to terms with how society is portraying people with disabilities. I was once part of an able society with my own negative perceptions about disability.

Undere
Deglon

P a r a p l e g i c

« Mes vacances de trois mois [en Grèce, ndlr] se sont prolongées sur trois ans. Puis soudain, tout a changé. J'ai eu un sérieux accident de voiture. Après une période en soins intensifs, j'ai passé du temps en rééducation, tentant de récupérer de mes importantes opérations du dos. J'ai été déclarée paralysée. »

Mariée, deux enfants.
Licence et diplôme en Éducation, Université de Western Cape.
Certificat de management en ressources humaines.
Master en Recherches psychologiques (Université de Cape Town).
Présidente directrice générale de l'entreprise « Disability Workshop Development ».

I was born as able-bodied girl in a small rural town called De Aar. I was mostly raised by my grandmother, as my mother was a nurse and needed to work long hours and sometimes night shifts. I spent the biggest part of my primary school years there, but at the beginning of my high school career, I was sent to school in Kimberley, which is quite near to De Aar. But it still meant that I spent a large part of my life travelling between the two towns. To a certain extent, this broadened my horizon and taught me that the world is smaller than we think.

I did fairly well at school and I liked the social activities like youth clubs, swimming, and modelling. I even participated in the occasional beauty pageant. I was a happy young girl with a lot of friends. After matric I moved to Cape Town to enrol in a teaching degree at the University of the Western Cape, and looking back, some of my most precious memories are those from my student days. Again, I did fairly well at university and during my final year the German department awarded me a scholarship to visit the Goethe Institute in Germany for a couple of weeks. The Goethe Institute teaches German at various levels to groups of non-German-speaking students.

I regard this very first trip overseas as the turning point in my life, as it awakened in me a deep interest in experiencing other countries, their language, architecture and cuisines. I found Germany fascinating, especially since I was there shortly after the collapse of the Berlin wall. Our group was quite diverse and consisted of French, Spanish, English and Greek students. As we were all away from home, we became a close-knit group and we spent most of our time together. I became particularly good friends with a Greek student who told me endless stories about the idyllic Greek islands, the Acropolis and Greek mythology.

After a few weeks in Germany, I returned home a changed person. I tried to resume my life, but shortly before my graduation ceremony in 1992, I decided to call my Greek friend. I packed my bags and went on holiday to Greece. There I got a job teaching English to high-school students, business people and hotel staff. Life was very comfortable and I quickly settled down, getting used to the beautiful beaches, the wonderful food and the island hopping. My three-month holiday dragged on for three years … But then suddenly everything changed. I was involved in a very serious car accident in Greece.

After an initial period in intensive care, I spent a further period of time recovering from major back surgery. I was declared paralysed.

As soon as I was in a stable condition, they transferred me from the Greek hospital to the Conradie Hospital's spinal cord unit in Pinelands, South Africa. There, my life consisted of nothing more than being woken up at 5 am to take a bath, and then to sit in my wheelchair waiting for half an hour of physiotherapy some time before lunch. After lunch, the same idle waiting followed for another half an hour of occupational therapy some time during the afternoon. Occasionally we had a guest speaker address us on issues like the benefits of tracksuit materials and soft sport shoes or how to look after your catheter to avoid pressure sores. I genuinely believed that my life as I knew it was over and I would never be human again.

Decisions about food, clothes, or how to spend my time were now made for me. The way I was treated made me feel like a total waste. My life had changed overnight and nobody bothered to emphasise that I would still be allowed to be me, except with a few adaptations here and there.

I still struggle to come to terms with how society is portraying people with disabilities. I was once part of an able society with my own negative perceptions about disability.

I mean, who doesn't remember the donation box in the form of a little girl with callipers, which one saw in all the major supermarkets? This was further reinforced by the change in other people's attitudes and behaviour towards me. Having lived a non-disabled life gave me that reference point: I knew what an average Saturday morning conversation at the check-out counter of Woolworths should sound like. Now I also know how these conversations differed from the conversations people have with the disabled. Even dear friends and acquaintances seemed to be patronising towards me; they just couldn't treat me the same way as before my accident.

My only link with reality was my boyfriend who had decided, come hell or high water, that our relationship would remain the same. His view at the time of the accident and ever since has been: 'You could have been either dead or in a wheelchair. I prefer the wheelchair, thanks.' His support made it much easier. Unfortunately though, you can't go through life clutching someone else's hand to affirm your identity or self-worth; it is something that has to start with you.

In time I came to realise that if you allow them to, people either knowingly or unknowingly impose their devalued sense of disability on you. I knew I had to learn how to reject and oppose this. While in rehabilitation I started rebuilding this devalued perception of myself. I became confident enough to say: This is who I am and this is how I demand to be treated. The onus was on me to oppose, challenge or redefine perceptions about me and my disability.

After the accident, I didn't even think about myself as a sexual being. I lost my identity because I was uncomfortable with my wheelchair and my flat shoes. As time went by and my self-acceptance grew, I became more confident. As a woman, sexual confidence starts with how you feel about yourself. You have to take charge of your emotions. Nobody else can do it for you.

So now, ten years later, I have gotten over myself. I know I am very attractive, I take great care of my appearance and I feel very confident. Like most other women I wish I was thinner, but luckily the feeling quickly passes. I am still with the same beloved partner that I had at the time of my accident, fifteen years ago. We are now married and we have two beautiful children together.

I have a fulfilling and demanding career, I love my children … and sometimes my husband has to beg for sexual attention (which he does quite shamelessly)!

Profile

Qualifications:
I have a BA from the University of the Western Cape, an H.Dip.Ed from the University of the Western Cape, a Human Resource Management Certificate and a Masters in Research Psychology from the University of Cape Town.

Occupation:
I am the Chief Executive Officer of Disability Workshop Development Enterprise (DWDE) in the area of poverty alleviation of people with disabilities.

Achievements:
I serve on the boards of directors of a number of organisations working in the area of economic empowerment of people with disabilities.

Contact details:
email: udeglon@artefact.co.za
cell: 082 749 0644
tel: 021 674 6139

Undera's album

Me as a little girl

A beauty queen

Graduation day

Topless on the beach

I was in a state of sheer panic thereafter, because I had not told him that I was a 'cripple'. This would also be my first date in my life.

« Le tout premier jour, alors que je me préparais à prendre mon déjeuner, mon employeur m'a appelé et m'a demandé de ne pas revenir travailler après le repas ni même les jours suivants. Ma seule collègue de bureau s'était plaint qu'en tant que personne infirme, je ne serais qu'une charge de travail supplémentaire pour elle. Elle lui avait lancé comme ultimatum de démissionner si je ne partais pas. »

Licence de Commerce (United Nation University - International Leadership Institute, Amman – Jordanie).
Position stratégique à GIBBS.
Réalise son master en Direction des Affaires (Université d'Afrique du Sud).
Responsable du développement des finances de «Breweries Afrique du Sud».
Directrice de « Eskom Holdings » et « DEC Holdings ».

Versha Rowjee
Spina bifida

To me it was a night of the stars. Even though I could only walk on crutches, the lights from the cameras flashed at my feet and there was a thundering applause.

Whenever I think back on my life, that night always stands out: my graduation ceremony at Wits University. With all the other graduates, I queued up and waited for my name to be called. I stood tall in all of my 1.3 metres and walked proudly across the stage to be 'capped and sashed'.

When the olive-coloured sash representing the Faculty of Commerce was placed over my shoulders, I was asked to turn and face the cameras for a picture. For that split second I felt like I was the centre of the universe and the whole world had stopped to honour me! That was a defining moment of my life and only the beginning of lots more to come.

For most of my friends and family it is expected that when you go to university you also gain a steady boyfriend or girlfriend, or even get engaged. However, when I was staying at the ladies' residence on campus, I only watched the other girls signing in their boyfriends when they came to visit. How I desired the same for myself, but alas, it never happened. For some reason I had many friends, both 'guys' and 'gals', but during all my years on university campus, I was never on a date, not once.

There were times when I felt very inferior and not good enough to be with someone. I knew that I was pretty and intelligent, but I was very aware of the fact that I was, after all, a cripple. So I silently watched the girls who had boyfriends with great envy and remember to this day how distraught I was when one of my friends got engaged during our final year. She was kind enough to realise that I wanted the same thing for myself, so she told me not to be so worried – my turn would come too. I believed her.

After my graduation I returned home to live with my parents. Even with a university degree in Commerce, my first job was as a data capturer: punching job cards all day long. Not surprisingly, I only lasted a few months in that job. I moved on to be a 'waste' clerk in a bank for a few weeks and then a manager's clerk. I stayed at the bank for over a year, but all the admin, routine and filing offered no job satisfaction. By the time I resigned, I felt very despondent, insecure and unsure about myself.

To make things worse, I felt like a total outcast on the social scene. I grew up as a Hindu in a very small Indian community. There were only four Hindu girls of the same age. We grew up together and went to school together. At this time in my life with my career going nowhere, it also happened that all three of these girls got married in the same year and within weeks of each other. It was a bitter pill to swallow. I was very competitive and did everything they did, but now I was out of the running. I felt like I was no longer worthy. I was angry and felt cheated out of not having what everyone else had, despite all my efforts to be normal.

The question I asked God and the universe was 'Why?' If I was never going to be the girl next door who gets married and lives happily ever after, then why could I not at least have a job that fulfilled me?

When I resigned from the bank I had no other job lined up, so I went on holiday to Mauritius with a widowed aunt. This trip opened a whole new world to me. The travel bug had bitten. I promised myself that I was going to travel to a different part of the world each year – a promise I kept. The experience also opened my mind to the possibilities of the bigger world out there and its wealth of wonderful people and opportunities. I knew that all I had to do was to keep my heart and my mind open to the possibilities of the universe and to receive these wholeheartedly.

Back home I started job hunting again, but it was a struggle because the open labour market was not receptive to people with disabilities. Even though I was overqualified and ambitious, I was prepared to settle for anything that would stimulate me and give me dignity. I kept on believing that something good would happen, and it did. The principal from the local school dropped by and asked if I would help out at the school. One of the teachers had to go on leave and he was in a difficult situation. He needed a teacher who could teach both English and Afrikaans to Grades 6 and 7. At first I laughed it off, but I still went to collect the books and reported for class the next Monday morning. Thus started another defining milestone of my life, the teaching experience!

I remember one specific moment as I was doing a comprehension lesson one morning, and a student asked me about something in the chapter we were reading. I answered it in the best and simplest way I could. I will never forget her response. She was in awe and said that she hoped that one day she would know as much as I did. I had learnt a very important lesson that would stay with me for the rest of my life: when you concentrate on yourself alone, you easily feel sorry for yourself and lose faith and confidence in your abilities, but once you start giving to people around you, you start appreciating yourself again.

That student made me appreciate myself again. So even though I initially thought that I was wasting my time being a teacher, I was there to learn from the students. My experience as a school teacher was a temporary one which was meant for me to be the student and not the teacher. After my teaching contract ended, I applied for a job as a bookkeeper for a small business. The owner was impressed with me, so I got the job. I was thrilled and the next morning I reported for work all excited, but that very first day as I was preparing to take my lunch hour, the owner called me in and asked me not to return after lunch and not to come back to work again. I did not do anything wrong and he had no problem with my work, but my only co-worker in the office had complained that as a disabled person, I would only add to her workload. The ultimatum she had put to him was that if I did not leave, she would.

At that point in my life I was very unaware of my rights and did not realise that I had a claim against them. I just left and went back home, but could not go into the house to face my mother and tell her that I had just been fired. So I just kept driving. I did not know where to go or what to do. Eventually I stopped my car in a parking lot and I cried. I wished for my life to end and felt so utterly worthless.

As I sat there crying, it dawned upon me that I had been living a lie. I thought that if I did everything that other people did, I would be normal like them. I had to face the truth: I was a person with a disability and the world saw me and treated me as one, no matter how much I denied it. I was born with a disability. And there for the first time, at the age of 25, I accepted that I was a disabled person.

I cannot remember how I got out of the parking lot or what mental and physical state I was in. I do remember updating my curriculum vitae, making several copies and sending them out to what was then known as the 'Big 5' auditing firms. About two months and several rejection letters later, I got an interview as well as a three-year contract. That was the longest I stayed in a job. It was a whole new beginning for me and I decided that I was going to be vibrant, strong and confident. I had to leave for work very early every morning, but I made sure that my hair and make-up was done every day and that I was dressed to the nines. I acknowledged myself and my confidence grew. My portfolio and client base grew and I was happy to dedicate my life to help build and support the clients I had grown with.

I developed a wonderful working relationship with the audit partner I reported to as well as with my fellow colleagues. Just when I thought I had my life and relationships totally figured out, I was challenged by another lesson. While completing a set of financial statements for a client, I was required to confirm a deposit balance with an outside company. I had to call the other company's head office to do the confirmation and started talking to a very friendly and charming young gentleman. He initially teased me, but then gave me the information I needed. In hindsight I was astounded when I'd realised that I teased him back. This was an affirmation of the confidence I felt.

First thing the next morning he called me and asked my out to lunch the same day. When I told him what a ridiculous idea that was, he insisted and continued to confirm our date.

I was in a state of sheer panic thereafter, because I had not told him that I was a 'cripple'. This would also be my first date in my life.

We went out to lunch, but I couldn't eat anything as my stomach was in knots, but we got along fine and talked a lot. He called me the next day, then a week later and then six months later and then I never heard from him again. I have no remorse or anger for the way things turned out; I still cherish the memory of that first date.

Remembering my second lesson in life, not to focus on myself, I started to get involved in organisations that served people with disabilities. These included social welfare programmes and one evening we met for a braai. There was another gentleman in a wheelchair. I met him and we mingled a bit that evening, but then he left without saying goodbye, which I thought was a bit abrupt. It was almost midnight when he called me on my cellphone. He asked me to please keep quiet because I apparently talked too much that evening, never allowing him to say anything. So I kept quiet. He said he wanted to tell me that he thought I was the most beautiful woman he had ever seen. I was shocked and totally confused at first.

From that moment onwards, there was no more doubt or debate: I was beautiful and the universe was showing this to me. None of the conversations with any of the men I mentioned above led to any long-lasting relationships. They were all like 'winks from God'. To this day, I have still not been in a steady relationship.

As I grow older I despair that I may not ever have the ideal 'normal' family, but as my romances continue, desire and wish is supported by hope and prayer.

Profile

Qualifications:
I hold a bachelor's degree in Commerce. I am an allumnus of the United Nations University, ILI in Amman, Jordan. I completed a Strategic Leadership Programme at GIBBS. I am currently busy with my master's in Business Leadership from Unisa.

Occupation:
I am a Development Accountant at South African Breweries. I hold two directorships, the board of Eskom Holdings Limited and the board of DEC Holdings (Disability Empowerment Concerns).

Hobbies:
I volunteer as secretary for the Association for People with Disabilities, I am treasurer for Shree Transvaal United Prajapati Society and serve on the Executive committee of the National Council for People with Physical Disabilities.

Contact details:
email: Versha.mohan@mweb.co.za
cell: 082 899 7117
tel: 011 234 6704

As I grow older I despair that I may not ever have the ideal 'normal' family, but as my romances continue, desire and wish is supported by hope and prayer.

My baby pictures!

Disability organisations and references ...

Western Cape Province

Name	Services rendered	Contact details
Association for the Physically Disabled PO Box 12982 Mowbray Cape Town 7705	Keeps a database of CVs of physically disabled candidates	Tel/Fax: +27 21 637 1204 Email: reable@iafrica.com
Association for the Physically Disabled PO Box 1544 Milnerton Cape Town 7435	Keeps a database of CVs of physically disabled candidates	Tel: +27 21 555 2881 Fax: +27 21 555 2888 Email: apd-wc@mweb.co.za
Association for the Physically Disabled PO Box 563 Goodwood Cape Town 7460	Keeps a database of CVs of physically disabled candidates	Tel: +27 21 592 4173 Fax: +27 21 592 4371 Email: tygerbergapd@mwebbiz.co.za Contact persons: Elzette Brown Mrs Gerber (CEO)
Deaf Federation of South Africa (DEAFSA) PO Box 226 Newlands Cape Town 7725	Keeps a database of CVs of hearing impaired/deaf candidates Advertises positions on its website: http://www.deafsa.co.za/index.asp	Tel: +27 21 693 4665/6 TTY: +27 21 683 4665 (Text phone) Fax: +27 21 671 2644 Email: deafsa@icon.co.za Email: deafsa2@iafrica.com Contact Person: L. Viljoen
Epilepsy South Africa (National Office) PO Box 73 Observatory Cape Town 7925	Keeps a database of CVs of candidates with epilepsy	Tel: +27 21 447 3014 (Head office) Tel: +27 21 703 9420 (Workshop) Fax: +27 21 448 5053 Email: nationaldirector.no@epilepsy.org.za
Fountain House 227 Lower Main Road Observatory Cape Town 7925	Keeps a database of CVs of mentally impaired persons Provides after-placement support Provides training for mentally impaired persons	Tel: +27 21 447 7409 Fax: +27 21 447 0319
Quadriplegic Association of the Western Cape PO Box 729 Durbanville Cape Town 7551	Keeps a database of CVs of physically disabled candidates	Tel: +27 21 975 6078 Fax: +27 21 975 5604 Email: qawc@absamail.co.za
Society for the Blind 45 Salt River Road Salt River Cape Town 7925	Assesses workstations and makes recommendations Maintains a database of CVs of visually impaired/blind persons Provides after-placement support Provides assistive technology Provides training for visually impaired/blind persons	Tel: +27 21 448 4302 Fax: +27 21 448 5206 Email: info@ctsb.org.za Contact person: Sarah Brock
Telkom (Pty) Ltd	Supplies the Teldem (Text phone) to communicate with deaf persons Supplies the Big Button CLI telephone for visually, hearing and physically disabled persons	Order line: 0800 119596 (It is best to go into your local Telkom office to order) Fax +27 12 325 3393
34 Degrees South 44 Berg-en-Dal 7600	Assists in the recruitment of personal assistants for people with spinal injuries Provides customised holidays in South Africa for people with spinal injuries	Tel: + 27 21 883 9409 Email: south@ananzi.co.za

Nthuse Management Staffing Solutions PO Box 23315 Claremont Cape Town 7735	Placement of disabled job candidates in various positions Specialists in recruitment of PWD* and Affirmative Action staff	Tel: +27 21 696 5198 Fax: 086 611 1833 Email: farinaaz@nthuse.co.za URL: www.nthuse.co.za

Ashley Gregory & Associates
PO Box 365
Edgemead
Cape Town
7407
	Placement of PWD in full- and part-time positions
	  Has a learnership programme for PWD
	  Specialises in bulk recruitment for PWD
	  Assists in a range of verification services
		Tel: +27 21 552 6960
		Fax: +27 21 555 4795
		Email: info@agarecruitment.com
		URL: www.agarecruitment.com

Vision Tree
Operational office:
35 Angelier Street
Door de Kraal
Bellville
7530
	Placement of PWD in various positions
	  Assists corporate or other companies with the selection and placement of PWD
	  Offers relevant training to PWD and companies employing PWD
		Tel: +27 21 910 4410
		Fax: 086 600 4410
		General queries:
		info@visiontree.co.za
		Booking queries:
		bookings@visiontree.co.za
		Hein Wagner (owner):
		hein@visiontree.co.za

Usizo Consulting
Postal address:
PO Box 758
Rondebosch
Cape Town
7700
	Places PWD nationally
	  General consulting services (job specs, interview guides, assessments etc.)
	  Development services
	  Placements of temporary staff for short-term contracts as well as permanent staff placements
		Tel: +27 21 532 3111
		Fax: + 27 21 532 3119
		Cell: 082 828 8438
		URL: www.usizoconsulting.co.za
		Contact person: Heather
		Contact person: Samantha
		Cell: 083 443 2874

Nadia Mason Personnel
Postal address:
PO Box 24008
Claremont
Cape Town
7735
	Placement of PWD
	  Placements of temporary staff for short-term contracts as well as permanent staff
	  Network with institutions and organisations to profile and recruit candidates with disabilities
		Tel: + 27 21 683 5895
		Email: nmp@nadiamason.co.za
		URL: www.nadiamason.co.za

Enabler website: Enabling jobs	Helps with placement of PWD in jobs Helps corporate or other companies with the selection and placement of PWD	Tel: +27 21 903 7860 Tel: + 27 21 797 6548 Email: info@enabler.co.za URL: www.enabler.co.za

Professional Disability Services
17 Pomela Crescent
Vredekloof Heights
Brackenfell
Cape Town
7560
	Renders disability employment services to employers
	  Conducts Disability Employment Sensitisation sessions
	  Conducts public-speaking services: conferences/events/corporates/government departments
	Compiles Disability Employment Policies & Procedures for employers
		Tel: +27 21 982 6044
		Cell: 082 990 7961
		Email: smitkaren@telkomsa.net
		Contact Person: Karen Smit

Disability Solutions PO Box 6037 Paarl 7620	Assesses workstations and makes recommendations Assists employers to obtain equipment and assistive technology	Tel: +27 21 872 1101 Fax: +27 21 872 9675 Email: guy@disabilitysolutions.co.za
Fimex Technologies PO Box 13113 Mowbray 7705	Supplies voice recognition software	Tel: +27 21 685 5051 Email: info@fimex.co.za
Dial-A-Ride PO Box 102 Observatory 7935	Transport for PWD Operates from 06h00 to 19h00	Tollfree number: 0800 600 89
Richard Cousins Pinelands	Performs vehicle modifications	Tel: +27 21 531 6857 Mobile: +27 82 368 3346
Cape Gateway 142 Long Street	Various accommodation options in the entire Western	Tel: 0860 142 142

*PWD stands for people with disabilities

Cape Town 8001	Cape region Accommodation choices to suit all needs of PWD Please consult their website for more details	Email: questions@ capegateway.gov.za URL: www.capegateway. gov.za/eng/directories/ facilities/47962
Blind SA Postal address: Private Bag X9005 Crown Mines Johannesburg 2025 Offices in: Cape Town Worcester	Offers bursaries Resources for members Braille services	Tel : + 27 21 422 8435 (Cape Town) Tel:+ 27 23 342 1579 (Worcester) Fax:+27 11 839 1217 Email: andresteyn7@telkomsa. net (Worcester) Email: avosloo1@telkomsa.net (Cape Town) URL: www.blindasa.org
Association for PWD, Western Cape Postal address PO Box 1544 Milnerton 7435 Physical address 2 Begonia Street Milnerton 7441	Offers information, advice and practical guidance for the following: • Transport • Day care • Sport and recreation • Roll-in Shop • Awareness • Fundraising • Employers/ recruitment	Tel: +27 21 555-2881/2/3/4 Fax: + 27 21 555-2888 Email: director@apd-wc.org.za URL: http://www.apd-wc.org. za Contact persons: Mrs Tessa Battinti (Knysna office) Tel: +27 44 382-0146 Mrs Irene De Bod (Worcester office) Tel: +27 23 347-2002
University of Cape Town (UCT) Private Bag X3 Rondebosch Cape Town 7701	Keeps a database of CVs of physically disabled candidates	Tel: +27 21 650 2427 Fax: +27 21 650 3794 Email: reinette.popplestone@ uct.ac.za URL: www.uct.ac.za Contact Person: Reinette Popplestone
University of the Western Cape Postal Address Private Bag X17 Bellville 7535	Keeps a database of CVs of physically disabled candidates Liaises with external recruiters as well as internal departments	Tel: +27 21 959 3586 Email: eabrahams@uwc.ac.za URL: www.uwc.ac.za Contact person: Evadene Abrahams

University of Stellenbosch Private Bag X1 Matieland Stellenbosch 7602	Liaises with external recruiters as well as internal departments Has a graduate placement programme	Tel: +27 21 808 3497 Fax: +27 21 808 4706 Email: cleophas@sun.ac.za URL: www.sun.ac.za Contact persons: Marcha Lyner-Cleophas, Mr Marquard (Head of Career office) Tel: +27 21 808 4705

Gauteng Province

Name	Services rendered	Contact details
Association for People with Disabilities (Johannesburg) Pallinghurst Road Westcliffe Johannesburg	Keeps a database of CVs of disabled candidates	Tel: +27 11 646 8331 Fax: +27 11 646 5248 Mobile: +27 83 247 7435 Email: simphawes@apdjhb. co.za Contact person: Siphawe Sele
Abacus Recruitment P O Box 4364 Rietvallei Pretoria 0174	Maintains a database of CVs of disabled candidates	Tel: +27 12 345 9200 Fax: +27 086 501 6822 Email: helouise@abacus.co.za Contact person: Helouise Conradie
Association for the Physically Disabled Private Bag x1 Parkview 2122	Social workers' services for PWD and their families Helps with coping mechanisms Attendant care services with daily physical needs like bathing, feeding, dressing etc. Protective workshops helping PWD to better their skills Daveyton Motivation & Assessment Centre for mothers and children under seven years Skyward Employment Services	Tel: +27 11 646 8331 Fax : +27 11 646 5248 Email: jeanettem@apdjhb. co.za

Brite Byte (PTY) Ltd
Postal address:
PO Box 2152
Highlands North
2037
Physical address:
162 8th Avenue
Highlands North
Johannesburg
	Specialises in the recruitment and placement of PWD
	   Majority of candidates are suitable for administrative, computer programming, contact centre and secretarial positions
	   Executive level candidates will be sourced if required
	Offers an end-to-end service
		Tel: + 27 11 440 0580
		Fax: + 27 011 440 0595
		Cell: 072 234 0343
		 Email: info@britebyte.co.za
		Contact person: Ashley Berman
		URL: www.britebyte.co.za
			National Accessibility Portal (NAP), SA
			PO Box 395
			Pretoria
				Has a list of 14 residential homes in the entire Gauteng region
				   Please consult website for specific details
					Tel: +27 12 841 2317
					Email: kchikane@csir.co.za
					URL: ww.napsa.org.za

Anix Lerato Disabled Placements
Postal address
P O Box 254
Florida, 1710
Physical address
1st Floor, Medical Centre
27 Goldman Street
Florida
	An agency catering exclusively for the placements of disabled persons in the marketplace	Tel: +27 11 472-7649
		Cell: 086 6321 761
		Email: anixlerato@mweb.co.za
			Thabo Mbeki Development Trust for Disabled People
			Physical Address:
			6th Floor,
			The Atrium
			41 Stanley Road
			Milpark
			Johannesburg
			
			 Postal address:
			PO Box 91006
			Auckland Park
			2006
				Fund mobilisation
				Grant making
				   Project and fund management
				   Support of innovative and effective development programmes
				   Support of appropriate advocacy activities
				   Promotion of strategic partnerships with other development organisations
					Tele: + 27 11 726 4481
					Fax: + 27 11 725 4479
					Email: admin@mbekitrust.co.za
					URL: www.mbekitrust.co.za

Neville Clarence Technologies PO Box 95309 Waterkloof Pretoria	Supply assistive technology for partially sighted, blind or deaf-blind candidates	Tel: +27 12 452 0380 Cell: 086 6321 761 Emergency Mobile (24 hrs): +27 82 669 0663 Email: info@nctec.co.za	**SA National Council for the Blind** Head Office: 514 White Street Bailey's Muckleneuk Pretoria	A network or organisations which collaborate towards securing the full participation and inclusion of the blind and partially sighted people in all areas of southern Africa	Tel: + 27 12 452 3811 Fax: + 27 12 346 4699 Email: admin@sancb.org.za URL: www.sancb.org

Saetra (Pty) Ltd
PO Box 25396
Monument Park
Pretoria
0105
	Offers various products and assessment tools
	   Some include: orthotics & prosthetics, linings & padding, fastenings & strapping
	   Please see the URL for more information
		Tel: + 27 12 345 3134
		Fax: + 27 12 345 1465
		e-mail: enquiry@saetrahealth.co.za
		URL: www.saetrahealth.co.za
			Blind SA
			Postal address:
			Private Bag X9005
			Crown Mines
			Johannesburg
			2025
			
			Offices in:
			Cape Town
			Worcester
				Offers bursaries
				Resources for members
				Braille services
					Tel : + 27 11 839 1793
					Fax: +27 11 839 1217
					Cell: 082 808 2812 (Pretoria)
					Cell: 082 962 9887 (Soweto)
					Email: dajvn@absamail.co.za (Pretoria)
					URL: www.blindasa.org

Independent Drive Systems PO Box 16379 Pretoria North	Installs the Easy Drive System in vehicles (adapts motor vehicles for people with disabilities)	Tel: +27 12 808 3447 Mobile: +28 82 853 0742 Email: ids1@absamail.co.za Email: tiaan.minnaar@absamail.co.za			

236

Name	Services rendered	Contact details
SA Sports Association for the Physically Disabled Postal Address: PO Box 751979 Gardenview 2047 Physical address: Disability House House 31, Rand Refinery Estate Refinery Road Germiston 1400	Sports include: table tennis, wheelchair basketball, cycling, power lifting, swimming, wheelchair rugby, wheelchair tennis Please visit their website for further details	Tel: +27 11 873 9191 Fax: 086 616 0694 Contact persons: Iris Cunningham (General manager) Email: iris@sasapd.org.za Nosipho Nkosi (Administrator) Email: nosipho@sasapd.org.za
University of Witwatersrand, JHB	Assisting companies to source final-year students for recruitment purposes	Tel: +27 11 717 9157 Fax: +27 11 403 1064 Email: Andrew.sam@wits.ac.za URL: www.web.wits.ac.za

KwaZulu-Natal

Name	Services rendered	Contact details
University of Kwa-Zulu Natal Please refer to website for details	Keeps a database of CVs of disabled candidates	Tel: + 27 31 260 1310 URL: www.ukzn.ac.za Contact person: Yanga Futshune (Disability coordinator)
AM Moola School Private Bag 09 Mount Edgecombe 4300	A day school for children with cerebral palsy from the age of 5 to 21 They offer speech and physiotherapy and have hostel facilities during the week	Tel: +27 31 500 3801
APD KwaZulu-Natal PO Box 561793 Chatsworth 3040	An association of social workers who council people with disabilities	Tel: +27 31 403 7041 Tel: +27 31 403 7074 apdkzn@cis.co.za
Arthur Blaxall PO Box 8132 Cumberwood 3235	This school caters for deaf, blind and partially sighted children from pre-primary to Grade 12 They have a day school and hostels only close for major public holidays	Tel: +27 33 387 1400 Email: blaxall@futurenet.co.za
Browns School Private Bag X 04 Ashwood 3605	This school caters for children with cerebral palsy and autistic children It ranges from Grade R to Grade 9	Tel: +27 31 700 3535 Email: browns@brownsschool.co.za
Bumbisizwe School Private Bag X 5005 Miadadeni 2951	This school caters for the physically disabled children from Grade R too Grade 7	Tel: +27 34 329 1214
Day Dawn Training Centre PO Box 19304 Dormerton 4015	This school caters for mentally disabled children from ages 7 to 18 Day school with three phases: junior, senior and intermediate	Tel: +27 31 207 1424

DEAFSA KwaZulu-Natal Deaf Associaton
180 Mansfield Road
Berea
Durban
4001
	This is a welfare association specialising in one-on-one counselling
	  Lifeskills training
	  Sign language education
		Tel: +27 31 201 2408
		Tel: +27 31 201 2261
		Fax: +27 31 202 7394
		Email: kznda@telkomsa.net

Disabled Children Action Group (DICAG) PO Box 3960 Durban 4000	Organisation dealing with mental and physical disability rights	Tel: +27 31 304 3555 Email: dicag@iafrica.com

Down Syndrome Association
382 Stella Rd
Malvern
Durban
4055
	An association offering support groups for parents with down syndrome babies
	  They send a support person to the parents on request
	  They have an up-to-date library with books, CDs and toys on how to stimulate the child's growth
	  They host fundraisers to help parents with down syndrome children
		Tel: +27 31 464 2055
		Email: downskzn@iafrica.com

Durban and Coastal Region Mental Health (SAFMH) PO Box 1206 Durban 4000	Mental health organisation	Tel: +27 31 207 2717 Email: dmhmail@dmh.co.za
Ekhuthuthukeni Special School PO Box 54541 Umlazi 4031	This day school caters for mentally disabled children Offers different workshops: junior, middle junior, pre-vocational and vocational	Tel: +27 31 907 5786 Fax: +27 31 907 2358
Entokozweni Special School PO Box 3028 Pietermaritzburg 3200	This day school caters for mentally disabled children Has different phases: foundation, intermediate and senior	Tel: +27 33 324 9046
Ethel Mthiyane Special School PO Box 370 Mandeni 4490	This day school caters for mentally and physically disabled children from Grades R to 9	Tel: +27 32 454 2230/8
Ethembeni School Private Bag X 1021 Hillcrest 3650	This is a school boarding school which caters for visually impaired and physically disabled children	Tel: +27 31 783 4718 Tel: +27 31 783 4568 Email: ethembeni@saol.com

Fulton School for the Deaf Private Bag 9002 Gillets 3603	School catering for deaf students	Tel: +27 31 767 1304 Tel: +27 31 767 1215 Email: fulton@iafrica.com Email: parkin01@mweb.co.z
Golden Gateway School 893 Bellair Rd Cato Manor 4091	This day school caters for the intellectually impaired from ages 7 to 18 It has three phases: junior, intermediate and senior	Tel: +27 31 261 2174
Harding Special School PO Box 441 Harding 4680	This school caters for physically disabled children from Grades 1 to 7 It has separate hostels for boys and girls	Tel: +27 39 433 1143 Email: hss@venturenet.co.za
KwaThintwa School for the Deaf Private bag X 1018 Hillcrest 3650	This is a boarding school for children aged 3 to 21 years and catering for Grades R to 11 Offers special skills training: hairdressing, woodwork and cookery	Tel: +27 31 783 4005 Email: mavisn@mweb.co.za
Natal Blind and Deaf Society PO Box 1109 Durban 4000	Blind and deaf services Please phone for more details	Tel: +27 31 309 4991 Email: fund.ndbs@telkomsa.net
Reunion School for Cerebral Palsy Children Private Bag C 32006 Mobeni 4060	This is a day and boarding school for cerebral palsy students from the ages of 6 to 21. It has three levels They also teach special skills like woodwork, gardening, baking and beadwork	Tel: +27 31 469 1094

Name	Services rendered	Contact details
uth African tional Council for e Blind (SANCB) Box 5970 rban 00	Council helping blind people with life skills, orientation development for young children, adult brail training and vocational training	Tel: +27 31 309 4991 Contact person: Mr Nair (principal) Email: jacenair@telkomsa.net
Giles Association r the Handicapped Box 38015 int 69	Association offering a gym for the handicapped Patients have to be referred by a doctor They have a charity shop to generate funds for the handicapped They also have workshops and employ between 85 and 90 handicapped people who do packing, sorting and labelling as well as a paperclip factory	Tel: +27 31 337 4404 Email: info@saintgiles.org.za

Eastern Cape Province

Name	Services rendered	Contact details
PD Port Elizabeth O Box 536 ort Elizabeth 00	Non-profit organisation that hosts workshops for the blind and physically disabled to better their skills	Tel: +27 41 484 5426 Email: may.daniels@apdpe.org.za Contact person: May Daniels
rcadia School rivate Bag X 9049 ast London 200	Primary school for learning disabled children from Grades 1 to 7	Tel: +27 43 743 5503 Email: root@arcadiaps.ecape.school.za
aysville Secondary chool rivate Bag X 9040 ast London 200	Secondary school for the mildly mentally disabled	Tel: +27 43 721 0270 Email: admin@baysville.co.za

Name	Services rendered	Contact details
Bergsig School Private Bag X 48 Uitenhage 6230	Secondary school for children with learning disabilities from Grades 8 to 10	Tel: +27 41 966 1130 Email: bergsig@netsurfers.co.za
Cape Recife High School PO Box 480 Port Elizabeth 6000	This school caters for children with learning disabilities and cerebral palsy, and who are partially deaf and partially blind, from Grades R to 12	Tel: +27 41 583 2147 Email: recife@interkom.co.za
College Street Primary School PO Box 497 East London 5200	The school caters for children from Grades R to 7 who are partially deaf and speech impaired The children wear hearing aids and learn to speak and lip read	Tel: +27 43 722 2247 Email: collegst@iafrica.com
DPSA 413 Oxford Street East London 5200	This member-based organisation caters for all disabled people They advocate for the rights of disabled people and have self-help projects as well as offer advice	Tel: +27 43 743 1579 Email: ec@dpsa.org.za Email: mncedisi@dpsa.org.za
Efata School for the Blind and Deaf PO Box 177 Umtata 5100	The school has two sections, one for the blind, which ranges from Grades R to 12, and thereafter they are informed about going to university or technicon The other section is for the deaf and ranges from Grades R to 9 After that they get their NCV or they can go further with skills development such as cookery, welding, bricklaying, carpentry and hairdressing	Tel: +27 47 536 0527 Tel: +27 47 536 0528 Tel: +27 47 536 0529 Email: efata@efata.ecape.school.za

Fumdisa Special School PO Box 1052 King Williamstown 5600	This school caters for mentally challenged children and has two phases: foundation and intermediate	Tel: +27 40 655 7856 Tel: +27 83 351 3854 The Principal Mrs Kiviti Email: fundisa65@mweb.co.za
Greenwood Primary School PO Box 12992 Centrahil 6006	This mainstream school has classes for the partially hearing and slow learners from Grades R to 7	Tel: +27 41 585 4142 Email: jhaysom@greenwoodschool.co.za
Happydale School PO Box 16149 Gelvandale 6016	This school is for the severely mentally disabled (day scholars) The scholars are divided into three groups: junior phase, middle phase and senior phase	Tel: +27 41 452 1240 Email: hendricks.craig@gmail.com
Kanyisa School for the Blind PO Box 11155 Algoa Park 6005	This school caters for partially and completely blind children from Grades R to 12	Tel: +27 41 485 3636 Tel: +27 83 270 6444 Phone at 11h00 Email: khanyisaschool@intekom.co.za
Khayalethu Special School PO Box 1457 East London 5200	This school caters for severely mentally impaired children from 6 to 18 years They have four groups: infant, junior, middle and senior	Tel: +27 43 722 4016 Tel: +27 82 654 9189 Contact person: Narieph Boshoff Email: ksschool@lautic.net
Kuyasa School for Severe Mental Handicap PO Box 826 Grahamstown 6140	This school caters for severely mentally impaired children who suffer from cerebral palsy from the age of 6 to 18 The principal evaluates all children before accepting them into the school	Tel: +27 46 622 6750 Email: jill@albanynet.co.za

Lonwabo School for Learners with Special Education Needs PO Box 11003 Algoa Park Port Elizabeth 6005	This school caters for all disabilities except the blind from Grades 1 to 7	Tel: +27 41 452 4227/8 Email: lonwbo@Xsubet.co.za
Parkland school PO Box 12177 Amalinda 5252	This school caters for mentally impaired children from 6 to 18 years They have three groups: junior, intermediate and senior	Tel: +27 43 748 5749 Email: speed@absamail.co.za

Efata School for the Deaf & Blind
PO Box 177
Umtata
5100
	This school caters for the deaf and blind
	   The blind section is from Grades R to 12
	   The deaf section is from Grades R to 12
	   Training is offered to be an electrician, bricklayer or carpenter
		Tel: +27 47 536 0527
		Fax: +27 47 536 0525
		Contact person: Ms Rasmeni

Port Elizabeth Deaf Association PO Box 12944 Central Hill Port Elizabeth 6000	This organisation caters for deaf, partly deaf and hard of hearing people They render social services which consist of hearing tests and assisting in family and social problems	Tel: +27 41 586 1189 Email: pedeafassoc@telkomsa.net
Quadpara Association for South Africa (QASA) PO Box 7947 Newton Park 6055	This is an information organisation for quadriplegics only They can direct a caller to the correct organisation for any assistance concerning medical consumables, wheelchair maintenance, cheap wheelchairs, grants and workshops	Tel: +27 41 364 2271/381 0964

Uitenhage Mental Health (SAFMH) PO Box 734 Uitenhage 6230	This organisation renders social and welfare services to all the mentally impaired people in their area	Tel: +27 41 922 8025 Email: minetteumh@ telkomsa.net
Disability Options	Assesses PWD Facilitates accessibility	Tel: +27 41 368 3707 Cell: 082 290 3764 Email: barndans@yebo.co.za Contact person: Tony Webb
Association for PWD, Nelson Mandela Bay & Cacadu District	Offers information, advice and practical guidance for the following: • Transport & accessibility thereof • Employers and recruitment specialists	Tel: +27 41 484 5426 Fax: + 27 41 484 7909 Email: info@apdpe.org.za URL: www.apdpe.org.za Contact person: Hans van de Haar (Executive director) Email: hans.vandehaar@ apdpe.org.za Cell: 082 441 3851

Northern Cape Province

Name	Services rendered	Contact details
Elizabeth Conradie School Private Bag X 5061 Southridge Kimberley 8300		Tel: +27 53 832 4354 Email: elcon@global.co.za
National Council for Persons with Physical Disabilities in SA (NCPPDSA) PO Box 928 Kimberley 8300	This council assists people with physical disabilities with contacting social workers, daycare, clinics, care attendance schemes, independent living centres, housing etc.	Tel: +27 53 833 3315 Tel: +27 82 926 5754 Email: elohim@mweb.co.za Email: apdnk@iafrica.com

Northern Cape Mental Health (SAFMH) PO Box 287 Kimberley 8300	This organisation employs mentally handicapped adults They have 13 different workshops for which the workers get paid	Tel: +27 53 841 0537
Retlameleng School for Disabled Children PO Box 2646 Kimberley 8300	This day school caters for the physically disabled, deaf, hard of hearing, partially sighted and blind Physically disabled and deaf children from Grades R to 7 Blind children from Grades R to 11	Tel: +27 53 871 3289 Tel: +27 53 871 1037 Email: retlameleng@ncape. school.za

Free State Province

Name	Services rendered	Contact details
Accessible Transport 47 Park Road Willows Bloemfontein 9320	Provides transport for persons with disabilities	Tel: +27 51 444 2883 Fax: +27 51 444 3443 Email: therina@apdfreestate. co.za Contact person: Dick Conradie
Association for the Disabled and the Deaf PO Box 20027 Willows Bloemfontein 9320	Keeps a database of CVs of disabled candidates Assesses employer's premises, buildings and workstations Provides after-placement support services	Tel: +27 51 444 2883 Fax: +27 51 444 3443 Email: sandra@apdfreestate. co.za Contact person: Sandra Goosen
Access One Stop PO Box 20027 Willows Bloemfontein 9320	Assesses employers' premises/ buildings	Tel: +27 51 448 4211 Fax: +27 51 444 3443 Mobile: +27 83 370 7243 Email: danie@apdfreestate. co.za Contact person: Danie Marais

Association for PWD Free State
Provincial Office
47 Park Road
Willows
Bloemfontein
9301
	Does awareness-raising on prevention of disabilities as well as on the potential, capabilities, challenges and needs of PWD
	  Promotes and maintains the integration of PWD into mainstream society
	  Empowers PWD by developing their potential and lobbying for equal opportunities
		Tel: + 27 51 444 2883/4
		Fax: + 27 444 3443
		Email: office@apdfreestate.co.za
		Cell: 082 440 7873
		Contact person: Ms Elzarie Devenish (Director)
		Email: elzarie@apdfreestate.co.za
		URL: www.apdfreestate.co.za

University of the Free State PO Box 339 Bloemfontein 9300	Assists with placement of students with disabilities Receives job vacancies from recruiters	Tel: +27 51 401 3713 Contact person: Roenelle Ceronio URL: www.uovs.ac.za
Amari School Private Bax X 67 Welkom 9460	This day school caters for mentally disabled children from 3 to 18 years	Tel: +27 57 352 8423 Email: amari@internext.co.za
Association for People with Disabilities (APD) PO Box 20027 Willows 9320	This association operates as a telephonic information centre which functions as the middle man between the government and PWD It provides all kinds of information for the physically disabled person	Tel: +27 51 444 2883 Tel: +27 51 444 2884 Tel: +27 51 444 1660 Email: therina@apdfreestate.co.za
Boitumelong School PO Box 1501 Garapulana 9775	This day school caters for mentally disabled children from age 6 to 21 and deals with the foundation phase	Tel: +27 51 874 1380
Deaf Club Bloemfontein PO Box 20027 Willows 9320	This club is formed by hearing impaired people who gather to attend sports and social events	Tel: +27 58 713 2821

Martie Du Plessis School PO Box 31895 Bloemfontein 9317	This day school caters for mentally and physically disabled children from 3 years to Grade 12 It also has hostels	Tel: +27 51 522 6801 Email: mdupschool@mdup.co.za
Mphatlalatsane School PO Box 847 Viljoenskroon 9520	This day school caters for mentally and physically disabled children from 3 years to Grade 12 It also has hostels	Tel: +27 56 343 0802 Email: mph2@telkomsa.net
National Council for Persons with Physical Disabilities (NCPPDSA) PO Box 13684 Noordstad Bloemfontein 9302	This council assists people with physical disabilities with contacting social workers, daycare, clinics, care attendance schemes, independent living centres, housing, and committees that assist with accessibility, work and employment, education, medical and motion and awareness	Tel: +27 51 436 7497 Email: webberm@iafrica.com
Nobilis School PO Box 118 Virginia 9430	Please contact the school for further details	Tel: +27 57 212 3833 Email: mwnobil@mweb.co.za
Northern Free State Mental Health (SAFMH) PO Box 434 Welkom 9490	This organisation deals with community work and marketing It also offers therapy, psychotherapy and refers clients to relevant organisations for medication	Tel: +27 57 352 1046 Email: nfsmh@internext.co.za
Thiboloha School for the Deaf and Blind Private Bag 829 Witsieshoek 9870	This school caters for the deaf from 4 years to Grade 10 and for the blind from 4 years to Grade 7	Tel: +27 58 713 0048 Tel: +27 58 713 2821 Email: thiboloha@lautic.net Mrs Steyn

| Tswellang School PO Box 16087 Bloemfontein 9307 | This day school caters for the physically disabled It offers Grades R to 9 It also has hostels It only takes children from the Free State | Tel: +27 51 432 3975 Email: tswellangcp@shisas.com |

Limpopo Province

Name	Services rendered	Contact details
DEAFSA PO Box 4989 Polokwane 0700	This organisation offers social services to the deaf that are usually offered by state departments, for instance assisting with applying for jobs and ID documents	Tel: +27 15 291 5248 Fax: +27 15 291 5227 Contact person: Mr Henry
Fulufhelo Special School PO Box 113 Sibasa 0970	This day school caters for severely and partially mentally impaired	Tel: +27 15 962 4732 Fax: +27 15 962 4037 Email: fulufhelo@absamail.com
SA Federation of Mental Health (SAFMH) PO Box 989 Tzaneen 0850	This is mainly a welfare organisation with social workers It has projects in villages and offers therapy to abused mentally disabled people	Tel: +27 15 307 5941 Email: safmhlp@telkomsa.net
Sidibeng School for the Deaf Private Bag X 9001 Ellisras 0555	This is a school for deaf children They have different levels and teach the children sign language from pre-school to Grade 10	Tel: +27 14 763 6130 Email: sidibengschool@lantic.net
Tshilidzini School for the Deaf Private Bag X 910 Shayadima 0945	This school caters for deaf children from the age of 5 until they complete Grade 7	Tel: +27 15 964 3197 Tel: +27 15 964 1022 Email: thusanang@mweb.co.za

North West Province

Name	Services rendered	Contact details
NWPG Office on the status of disabled people Private Bag X 129 Mmabatho 2735	This organisation is part of the state department that monitors all the services and projects that are done for disabled people like housing and computer libraries	Tel: +27 18 387 3007 www.nwpg.gov.za
M.M. Sebitloane Special School Private Bag X 1008 Taung Station 8580	This day school caters for the mentally disabled It takes children from the age of 7 years to 15 years	Tel: +27 53 994 1666 Tel: +27 53 994 1653 Contact person: Mr Sebiploane
Mafikeng Deaf Club PO Box 2056 Ottosdal 2610	This club is formed by hearing impaired people who gather to attend sports and social events	Tel: +27 18 571 0826
Meerhof School Private Bag X 354 Hartbeespoort 0216	This school caters for the physically disabled They offer Grade R to 12 (18 years) They also have pre-career classes for slower learners	Tel: +27 12 259 1241 Email: meerhofskool@absamail.co.za
Phelang Special School PO Box 1123 Hammanskraal 0400	This school caters for mentally disabled as well as physically disabled children	Tel: +27 12 717 4697
Quadpara Association of SA (QASA) PO Box 6404 Flamwood 2572	This is an information organisation for quadriplegics. They can direct a caller to the correct organisation for any assistance concerning medical consumables, wheelchair maintenance and cheap wheelchairs, and assist with grants and workshops	Tel: +27 18 468 8303

With the help and love of ...

Lucie Pavlovich

Photographer

Lucie Pavlovich (photographer) was born in Prague. After a successful career as an international model she attended London University, graduating with a BA (Hons) in Politics and Psychology. Her friend, celebrity photographer Terry O'Neill, introduced her to the world behind the camera. During an internship with him, she began to understand that this was where her natural passion and talent lay, leading to her career as a fashion and glamour photographer.

When Marlene le Roux invited Lucie to become involved in the concept of producing a book celebrating the beauty and sensuality of disabled women, she was immediately at-tracted to the idea. With her long experience in front of the camera, and being a woman herself, she was able to relax the ladies into showing the camera their innate beauty and positivity – and they in turn found it a rewarding and liberating experience. Lucie says: 'To help these ladies realise a dream was one of the most inspirational experiences of my life, and I am very grateful to them for that opportunity.'

So often I encounter people with a deep, embedded prejudice to disabled femininity, surprisingly even children (innocently reflecting the views they are taught), and I see that through this book we have opened the door a little, that has been so firmly closed for too long. I have met many people (abled or disabled) that have found the lives of these ladies to be immensely inspirational and I have received so much gratitude that I can only pass on to all the actual stars of this book.

Well done ladies, you have been through so much and you truly are beautiful.

Contact details:

Email: lucie@luciepavlovich.com

http://www.luciepavlovich.com

145

T o y
McMaster
H a i r   s t y l i s t

Toy McMaster was trained as a hair stylist in Durban. He travelled to the UK where he started his career and very quickly became sought after.

He returned to South Africa and opened his own salon in Cape Town. The salon has enjoyed great success.

He believes his passion for hair, people and shifting boundaries gives him the edge.

He volunteered to get invloved in this project, donating his time, skills and products.

Toy says: 'The great thing about hair is how it can change someone within seconds and it can give you such a wonderful confidence boost. It was great to see the effect a change of hair can have on someone while working with these women.

'I think one of the most touching moments was hanging out with Bonita on the last day of the shoot and just being amazed at how incredibly strong and positive she is. Like all the other ladies! They make us look disabled by just living their lives so fully.'

Contact details:

Cell: 079 776 6313

Tel: 021 553 3926

Email: mc_mac79@yahoo.co.uk

A n d r i e
Nieuwoudt
M a k e - u p   a r t i s t

After a few years in the tourism industry, Andrie Nieuwoudt decided to follow her passion. She always had a keen interest in make-up and how it accentuates a person's natural beauty.

She started working as make-up artist in Cape Town, trained in various beauty therapies.

She was excited to get involved in this book, and looked forward to the challenge and difference it would bring. 'I was amazed at how easy it was to turn these women into gorgeous ladies. They are so naturally beautiful.'

She says: 'I will never forget the moment after Marlene and Jonida's shoot, when her able-bodied daughter told her mom she never thought she could be jealous of her mom, but she was, and she had never seen her mom as beautiful and confident as that day.'

Contact details:

Cell: 072 463 0423

Tel: 021 553 3926

Email: an3@webmail.co.za

Mandy Barnes

Project manager

'I first heard about Marlene's vision for the book about two years ago and thought that it was a brilliant idea, so when she asked me to get involved, I jumped at the opportunity. I believe in the importance of doing work that stirs your passion, makes a difference and that helps you to connect with your higher purpose. I firmly believe that working on this book enabled me to fulfil these ideals.

'I acted as project manager and my task was mainly to connect with all the potential candidates for the book. This meant following up initial contacts, and sharing the vision of the book in a way that would make them interested, excited and want to commit to this incredible process. I recall my own level of excitement each time one of the women responded positively to the invitation to get involved.

'And as the women submitted their stories, the true impact of this book, not only on the participants, but on their families and all those involved in the process, became evident. Here we had 23 women, 'who each in her own way, transcended the limitations and narrow definitions society tends to place on women with disabilities. Each one overcame obstacles and adversity and in the process reclaimed their rights to femininity, beauty, motherhood and womanhood. Their strength, courage, determination, resilience, passion, energy, sense of humour and mostly, zest for life, sustained me throughout the process of keeping the detail together, and continues to inspire me.

'My involvement in this process enhanced my awareness of many challenges and barriers people with disabilities continue to encounter daily. It is through engaging with people as people first, and then people who happen to have a disability, that we begin to break down our own misconceptions and prejudices.'

Amanda Barnes is a learning and development consultant who has extensive experience in training, consulting, research, facilitation and project management in both public and private sectors.

She holds a BA (Psychology) and a BA Hons (Development Studies) from UWC and an MPhil in Social Policy, Planning and Administration from UCT.

Contact details:

Email: mandybarnes@iafrica.com

Michael de Beer

Coordinator

Michael de Beer is the Marketing Coordinator of Artscape's Audience Development and Education department. He has worked variously in the clothing industry for both men's retail and ladies' manufacturing, in marketing and public relations, as a fashion stylist, art director and photographer, in the F&B industry locally and internationally, and has worked as a tour guide in South Africa.

'Marlene often mentioned this book as a longstanding dream. Finally Genugtig! Publishers saw the opportunity to implement this project with vision, dedication, empathy and understanding. Personally I went straight into action with 'connecting' with the ladies, knowing the overall outline and desired results of my brief. During my 'people' career, I've engaged with persons from all walks of life. Until I came face-to-face with this amazing group of ladies, one only thinks you understand disability and/or affliction. We are all 'normal' people in every sense of the word, capable, thinking, versatile, fun, loving, thinking, caring, the words are endless. I took a step back, taking stock, to look at myself as a human being, how as able bodies, we have naught to complain about. Energy radiated from all on the photo shoots, emotions were high, sometimes tearful yet always satisfying. I'd do it all over again!'

Contact details:

Email: info@madb.co.za

Zimkhita Melody Kana

Researcher

Zimkhitha Melody Kana holds a Diploma in Business Management from Cape Peninsula University of Technology. She is a registered student at Unisa studying towards a BA in Literature and Linguistics.

Contact details:

Email: zimkhithak@artscape.co.za

Jo-Anne Peterson

Researcher

Jo-Anne Peterson is a multi-faceted artist energetically driven by experiences gained in theatre production, magazine journalism, performance art, event coordination, hip hop activism, radio talk-show presenting as well as TV show hosting.

Clothing & *locations*

Thank you to Richard of Hip Hop for his enthusiasm and providing us with clothing for the shoots.
http://www.hiphopfashion.co.za

Thank you to Vigilla of Diesel for supporting this book and for providing clothing from Diesel.
http://www.diesel.com

And thanks to Ruth and Catherine from Bead Merchants for providing us with the stunning beads.
http://www.beadm.co.za

Thank you to the following beautiful places for allowing us to use their hotels and guesthouses for our shoots:

Primi Seacastle
13 Victoria Road, Camps Bay, South Africa
Tel: +27 21 438 4010
Fax: +27 21 438 4015
http://www.primi-seacastle.com

27 on First in Campsbay
27 1st Crescent, Camps Bay, Cape Town, South Africa
Tel: +27 21 438 0163
Fax: +27 21 438 9310
Cell: +27 83 234 9987
Skype us: twentysevenonfirst
http://www.twentysevenonfirst.co.za

Greenways Hotel
No.1 Torquay Avenue, Upper Claremont, Cape Town, South Africa
Tel: +27 21 761 1792
Fax: +27 21 761 0878
E-mail: info@greenways.co.za
http://www.greenways.co.za

A special thanks to Catherine Ritchie and everyone at the Mount Nelson.

Cape Town's most famous hotel, the Mount Nelson is an urban sanctuary set in tranquil gardens on the lower slopes of Table Mountain, offering an oasis of stylish sophistication, privacy and tranquility.

The 201 luxurious rooms and suites offer garden or mountain views and leisure facilities include two heated swimming pools, floodlit tennis courts, a luxurious spa, a private gymnasium, golf practice net and high-speed Internet access throughout the hotel. The extensive grounds also make the hotel a haven for young families.

Alfresco health-focused lunches can be enjoyed in Oasis restaurant as well as elegant dinners in the Cape Colony restaurant, which offers a contemporary menu with an Asian twist and an award-winning wine list. Guests can also indulge in decadent Afternoon Teas served daily in the Lounge or sip champagne by night in the stylish Planet Champagne and Cocktail Bar, which spills out onto a magnificent garden terrace beneath the beautiful African night sky.

Located just a short stroll from the historic city centre and within close proximity to the V&A Waterfront, the hotel also offers easy, close access to Cape Town's best beaches and is situated just 20 minutes from Cape Town International Airport.

76 Orange Street, Cape Town, South Africa
Tel: +27 21 483 1737
Fax: +27 21 483 1001
Email: reservations@mountnelson.co.za
http://www.mountnelson.co.za

Special thanks & acknowledgements

Special thanks

This book would not have been possible if I had not had the help of a passionate and absolutely remarkable person like Amanda Barnes, who had the characteristics of being patient, but above all, a belief in and love for people. Her absolute professionalism and highly experienced project management skills pulled this book through.

The vision of this book – the stories and sensual photographic displays – was made possible through an understanding of women's bodies, the absolute understanding of what we needed to achieve and pushing the boundaries constantly for high quality. The artistic photography makes this book a special edition. I was privileged to work with a passionate, highly qualified and internationally renowned photographer like Lucie Pavlovich.

Vera and Jackie Nagtegaal believed in the realisation of this book from the beginning. They were God-sent at a time when no one wanted to touch or commit to this publication. They are publishers with a difference because they understand adversity and their main aim is to put stories that can make a difference into the public arena. They have enriched and touched my life in so many ways. Thank you for your unconditional belief in this book and in the good of other people.

Michael de Beer ensured that all the detail and the final arrangements for the photo shoots and logistics to get the women to locations were taken care of. Your support throughout this process means a great deal to me.

Zimkhitha Kana and Jo-Anne Petersen spent many hours researching and contacting various disability organisations around the country, some in the remote, rural areas.

To Michael Maas and the Artscape team, thank you for allowing Artscape to be part of this project. Your leadership and utmost belief in giving people opportunities is admirable.

Thank you to everyone from Photohire and ORMS Photolab for your support.

Special acknowledgement to

Simeon, my husband, for taking care of the children and support in finding myself.

My mom-in-law Valerie George; thanks for always being there for me.

Eric Miller as professional photographer, who affirmed the project from the outset.

All my lovers who looked at me!

Yolanda and Mynie, Adam's nurses, for taking such good care of my son.

Robert Prince, for helping me with the compilation of the first proposal.

Lucia Hess, as a friend, who has from the inception urged me to complete this book.

Niel le Roux: when I despaired in finding a publisher, you connected me to the Nagtegale. I am eternally grateful.

Tarnia van Zitters for the wonderful food.

Trevor MacPherson is an absolute gem, who made us all feel special and captured this whole process on camera.

Lexie, in his quiet way made us all feel like fashion models and desirable.

Toy and Andrie who turned all of us into goddesses. You are incredible!

With love,
Marlene le Roux

153

'Just because you are blind, and unable to se

ny beauty doesn't mean it does not exist.'
Margaret Cho

First published in South Africa in 2008

Published by Genugtig! Publishers (Pty) Ltd
Lipco Chambers, Village Walk, Parklands, 7441, Cape Town, South Africa

Photographs © Lucie Pavlovich

All stories remain the property of the authors

Compilation © Marlene le Roux

Publication © Genugtig! Publishers

Design & Layout Genugtig! Publishers

Proofreading by Bronwyn McLennan

Hair styling by Toy McMaster, except for the styling of Sebenzile, Barenice and Gillian,
which was done by Wonita Koopman

Make-up by Andrie Nieuwoudt, except for Sebenzile, Barenice and Gillian,
which was done by Burnodette Wood

Art direction by Lexie (www.lexie.co.za) and Lucie Pavlovich (www.luciepavlovich.com)

O.K. per Deanna Flores 6/29/2011

ISBN 978-0-9802606-7-0